SOUNDS, SYMBOLS AND SPELLINGS

Adam Brown

National Institute of Education
Nanyang Technological University

Singapore • Boston • Burr Ridge, IL • Dubuque, IA • Madison, WI • New York • San Francisco
St. Louis • Bangkok • Bogotá • Caracas • Kuala Lumpur • Lisbon • London • Madrid
Mexico City • Milan • Montreal • New Delhi • Santiago • Seoul • Sydney • Taipei • Toronto

The McGraw-Hill Companies

Sounds, Symbols and Spellings

1 2 3 4 5 6 7 8 9 10 SEP 09 08 07 06 05

When ordering this title, use ISBN 007-124772-6

Printed in Singapore

Contents

Figure

Tables

Tasks

Symbols for British English phonemes 

Vowels

Symbol	as in	Symbol	as in
/iː/	*bean, deed, feel, leave, sleep*	/ɜː/	*bird, herb, stir, turn, foreword*
/ɪ/	*bin, did, fill, live, slip*	/ə/	*about, doctor, surprise, forward*
/e/	*beg, Ellen, lend, revel, text*	/eɪ/	*faint, made, page, stay, train*
/æ/	*bag, Allan, land, ravel, taxed*	/aɪ/	*file, fly, quite, tribe, wide*
/ʌ/	*budge, chum, done, grunt, tusk*	/ɔɪ/	*boil, choice, coin, noise, toy*
/ɑː/	*barge, charm, darn, grant, task*	/əʊ/	*home, rogue, rose, toad, though*
/ɒ/	*copse, not, moss, potter, spot*	/aʊ/	*brown, found, house, loud, now*
/ɔː/	*corpse, nought, Morse, porter, sport*	/ɪə/	*cheery, feared, fierce, here, weird*
/ʊ/	*full, look, pull, should, soot*	/eə/	*bear, fares, hair, scared, where*
/uː/	*fool, Luke, pool, shooed, suit*	/ʊə/	*cure, during, poor, pure, tour*

Consonants

Symbol	as in	Symbol	as in
/p/	*pack, pause, crumple, lap, rope*	/s/	*seal, fussy, racer, false, piece*
/b/	*back, bores, crumble, lab, robe*	/z/	*zeal, fuzzy, razor, falls, peas*
/t/	*tennis, atom, bolt, cent, abort*	/ʃ/	*Confucian, mission, rush, shoe*
/d/	*Dennis, Adam, bold, send, aboard*	/ʒ/	*confusion, pleasure, usual*
/k/	*calorie, creak, anchor, decree, lock*	/h/	*hello, hot, behave, who, whole*
/g/	*gallery, Greek, anger, degree, log*	/m/	*moon, motion, smug, ram, sum*
/tʃ/	*chain, cheer, choke, lunch, rich*	/n/	*noon, notion, snug, ran, sun*
/dʒ/	*Jane, jeer, joke, lunge, ridge*	/ŋ/	*monkey, rang, sung, thing*
/f/	*few, fine, safer, leaf, proof*	/l/	*lack, lay, bland, allows, teller*
/v/	*view, vine, savour, leave, prove*	/r/	*rack, ray, brand, arouse, terror*
/θ/	*thigh, think, nothing, truth, myth*	/w/	*whack, woo, what, queen, twelve*
/ð/	*thy, this, father, soothe, clothe*	/j/	*yak, you, yacht, queue, stew*

Preface

The purpose of this book is to respond to the expressed need of learners for material helping them to become familiar with the phonemic symbols used in British dictionaries and phonetics books. The focus is on perception, that is the ability to work out from a phonemic transcription in a dictionary what sounds a particular word has, and the tasks contained in this book are aimed at this perceptual aspect. Nevertheless, practice in perception is likely to lead to an improvement in production, that is the ability to transcribe words.

It is not the purpose of this book to try to teach phonetics. Obviously we need to establish the contrasting units of pronunciation before we can relate these sounds to their phonemic symbols, and therefore a basic description of English sounds is necessary. However, any reader who wishes or needs to investigate the articulation of English sounds in greater depth is encouraged to read a standard British phonetics textbook, such as Roach (2000), Cruttenden (2001).

Nor is it the purpose of this book to describe the correspondences between English sounds and spellings in great detail. This is obviously an important part of acquiring the ability to read and write in English, as well as the ability to transcribe English sounds accurately. An outline of the main sound-to-letter correspondences is given in Chapter 1, and an introduction to the main points relating to literacy is given in Chapter 9. Readers wishing to delve deeper into these aspects should consult books on the subject, such as Carney (1994) for spelling, and Kern (2000) and Holme (2004) for literacy.

It is envisaged that many readers of this book will be non-native learners of English, or non-native or native students on phonetics courses. Those readers who are teachers of English can use the book not only to improve their ability at reading phonemic transcriptions, but also to help them in their English language teaching. Several of the tasks in the book can be used in the classroom, after adaptation to the age and level of the students.

Tasks

Tasks have been included in many chapters. The purpose of these tasks is for readers to give some thought to the sounds of English, and to be able to divorce sounds from spelling. It is important that you should attempt the task questions before consulting the answer key. Otherwise, you will not be actively trying out English transcription and learning from your mistakes, but merely be passively taking in information.

The tasks are shown by a large question mark icon.

The key icon indicates that the task comes with an answer key. The answer key is at the back of the book starting on page 121. Only the correct answers are usually transcribed, unless there is a need to point out some feature of the incorrect answers. If necessary, look up the transcription of incorrect guesses in a reputable British dictionary or, more specifically, a pronouncing dictionary. The two major British English pronouncing dictionaries are:

Wells, J. C. (2000) *Longman Pronunciation Dictionary.* (2nd ed.) Harlow: Pearson Education.

Roach, P., Hartman, J. & Setter, J. (Eds. 2003) *English Pronouncing Dictionary.* (16th ed.) Cambridge and New York: Cambridge University Press (the descendant of the Daniel Jones *English Pronouncing Dictionary*).

This icon shows that a recording of the words or passage is contained on the audio CD that accompanies this book. The contents of the CD are listed on page 161.

This icon gives suggestions on how some of the tasks may be modified. Teaching tips and advice for readers who are teachers of English are also provided here.

The intended readership of this book ranges from non-native learners (at all levels from beginner to advanced) to native speakers of English. As a result, the tasks in the book differ in their difficulty level, from easy to tough. Readers at lower levels should try not to be disheartened that some of the tasks are too difficult, for instance, in terms of the depth of vocabulary required. At the other extreme, native speakers may find some of the tasks rather elementary and unchallenging.

Conventions

In this book, following standard linguistic convention:

- letters of the alphabet and words in spelling are printed in italics, eg the letter *a, girl*
- sounds (phonemic transcription) are printed in slant brackets, eg /ə, gɜːl/
- the meanings of words and expressions are printed in quote marks, eg 'female child'

Acknowledgements

I would like to thank the following people, who have all contributed to this book in some way:

- My students, past and present, whose anxiety over using phonemic symbols was the impetus for writing this book, and who have wittingly or otherwise been guinea-pigs for the tasks
- The following people, who read drafts of the book: David Deterding; Valerie Yule; Doug Everingham; my children, Nadiah and Hamzah, aged 12 and 10 (who found most of the tasks easy-peasy)
- Tom McArthur, for permission to use Strevens' diagram (page 46)
- Heather Kay, for lending her voice to the CD recording
- The McGraw-Hill editors and proofreaders

Dedication

For Chris Upward, deviser of Cut Spelling, who reminded me why English spelling is a dog's dinner and aroused my interest in spelling reform

1

Consonant and vowel sounds

This chapter introduces the consonant and vowel sounds of English. These are collectively known as the segments, in contrast to suprasegmental features of pronunciation, such as intonation and rhythm. Suprasegmentals are not treated in this book, because they are not represented in the transcriptions found in dictionary entries. However, they should not be overlooked in any course on pronunciation, as they contribute to overall intelligibility.

Consonant sounds are defined as ones that involve an obstruction in the mouth during their production, as opposed to vowel sounds, which have little or no obstruction. There are 24 consonant sounds, and 20 vowel sounds in the British accent of English used as a reference in this book. The procedure whereby we arrive at the figures of 24 and 20 is explained in Chapter 3.

Consonants

There are 24 consonant sounds in British English, and in most accents of English worldwide. What follows is a list of the symbols for those sounds, each with a brief description of how the sound is produced, and of the main sound-to spelling correspondences (from Carney, 1994).

Plosives

Plosives are made by bringing the articulators into complete closure so that air does not escape through the mouth, and preventing air from escaping through the nose, by closing the velum (soft palate). There are six plosives in English, three pairs of voiceless and voiced equivalents.

The sound /p/ is a voiceless bilabial plosive. The lips are brought together, and the vocal cords are not vibrating. The main sound-to-spelling correspondences are given on page 2.

The sound /b/ is a voiced bilabial plosive. It is thus the same as /p/, but the vocal cords are vibrating.

Phoneme	Spelling	% of the time in connected speech	Example words
/p/	*p*	95	*pan*
	pp	5	*copper*
/b/	*b*	98	*bit*
	others	2	

The sound /t/ is a voiceless alveolar plosive. The tongue tip and/or blade touches the alveolar ridge, and the vocal cords are not vibrating.

The sound /d/ is a voiced alveolar plosive. It is thus the same as /t/, but the vocal cords are vibrating.

Phoneme	Spelling	% of the time in connected speech	Example words
/t/	*t*	96	*ten*
	tt	3	*pattern*
	others	1	
/d/	*d*	98	*dame*
	dd	2	*sudden*

The sound /k/ is a voiceless velar plosive. The tongue back touches the velum, and the vocal cords are not vibrating.

The sound /g/ is a voiced velar plosive. It is thus the same as /k/, but the vocal cords are vibrating.

Phoneme	Spelling	% of the time in connected speech	Example words
/k/	*c*	59	*car*
	k	21	*king*
	ck	6	*back*
	others	14	
/g/	*g*	92	*go*
	gu	3	*guess*
	gg	2	*ragged*
	others	3	

Affricates

For the two affricates in English (/tʃ, dʒ/), a large area of the tongue, comprising parts of the blade and front, touches a large area of the roof of the mouth, comprising parts of the alveolar ridge and hard palate. After the initial complete closure, the tongue lowers with a hissing noise (frication).

The sound /tʃ/ is a voiceless palato-alveolar affricate. The vocal cords are not vibrating. (*Palatalisation* is the process of an original /t, d, k, s, z/ coalescing with a following /iː, j(uː)/ to give the palato-alveolar sounds /tʃ, dʒ, ʃ, ʒ/, eg *combustion, soldier, logician, repulsion, closure.*)

The sound /dʒ/ is a voiced palato-alveolar affricate. It is thus the same as /tʃ/, but with vocal cord vibration.

Phoneme	Spelling	% of the time in connected speech	Example words
/tʃ/	*ch*	65	*chest*
	tch	10	*match*
	others	25	Palatalisation, eg *question, ritual*
/dʒ/	*g, ge, dge*	71	*gem, page, badge*
	j	29	*jug*

Fricatives

Fricatives are produced by bringing one articulator close to another, but not touching. As the air escapes through the small gap that has been left, a hissing noise (frication) is caused. There are nine fricatives in English (four pairs of voiceless/voiced correspondents, and /h/).

The sound /f/ is a voiceless labio-dental fricative. The lower lip comes towards (the front face of) the upper teeth, causing frication. The vocal cords are not vibrating.

The sound /v/ is a voiced labio-dental fricative. It is thus the same as /f/, but with vocal cord vibration.

Phoneme	Spelling	% of the time in connected speech	Example words
/f/	*f*	84	*fat*
	ph	11	*phone*
	ff	4	*offer*
	others	1	
/v/	*v*	100	*very*

The sound /θ/ is a voiceless dental fricative. The tongue tip and/or blade comes towards (the back face of) the upper teeth, causing frication. The vocal cords are not vibrating.

The sound /ð/ is a voiced dental fricative. It is thus the same as /θ/, but with vocal cord vibration.

Phoneme	Spelling	% of the time in connected speech	Example words
/θ/	*th*	100	*thigh*
/ð/	*th*	100	*then*

The sound /s/ is a voiceless alveolar fricative. The tongue tip and/or blade comes towards the alveolar ridge, causing frication. The vocal cords are not vibrating.

The sound /z/ is a voiced alveolar fricative. It is thus the same as /s/, but with vocal cord vibration.

Phoneme	Spelling	% of the time in connected speech	Example words
/s/	*s, ss*	79	*sit, dress*
	c	15	*cent*
	others	6	
/z/	*s*	93	*rise*
	z, zz	5	*zero, jazz*
	others	2	

The sound /ʃ/ is a voiceless palato-alveolar fricative. As for the affricates /tʃ, dʒ/, a large area of the tongue, comprising parts of the blade and front, comes towards a large area of the roof of the mouth, comprising parts of the alveolar ridge and hard palate, causing frication. The vocal cords are not vibrating.

The sound /ʒ/ is a voiced palato-alveolar fricative. It is thus the same as /ʃ/, but with vocal cord vibration.

Phoneme	Spelling	% of the time in connected speech	Example words
/ʃ/	*sh*	37	*ship*
	ch	1	*chef*
	others	55	Palatalisation, eg *dictation, repulsion, logician*
	others	7	
/ʒ/	*s*	91	Palatalisation, eg *occasion*
	g	4	*beige*
	others	5	

The sound /h/ is a voiceless glottal fricative. The two vocal cords come towards each other, causing frication. Since this primary articulation for /h/ involves the vocal cords coming towards each other, they cannot also be vibrating for voice: /h/ is thus considered voiceless.

Phoneme	Spelling	% of the time in connected speech	Example words
/h/	*h*	99*	*home*
	wh	1*	*whole*

* Estimates (percentages not given by Carney)

Nasals

Nasals are made by bringing the articulators into complete closure so that air does not escape through the mouth, but allowing air to escape through the nose, by opening the velum. There are three nasals in English. They are all voiced.

The sound /m/ is a voiced bilabial nasal. The lips are brought together; air escapes through the nose, and the vocal cords are vibrating.

The sound /n/ is a voiced alveolar nasal. The tongue tip and/or blade touches the alveolar ridge; air escapes through the nose, and the vocal cords are vibrating.

The sound /ŋ/ is a voiced velar nasal. The tongue back touches the velum; air escapes through the nose, and the vocal cords are vibrating.

Phoneme	Spelling	% of the time in connected speech	Example words
/m/	*m*	96	*money*
	mm	3	*summer*
	others	1	
/n/	*n*	97	*need*
	nn	1	*tunnel*
	others	2	
/ŋ/	*ng*	75 *	*sing*
	n	25 *	*sink*

* These figures do not include the common *-ing* inflection.

Lateral

For /l/, the only lateral in English, the tongue tip touches the alveolar ridge in the centre, air escapes over the sides of the tongue without frication, and the vocal cords are vibrating.

Phoneme	Spelling	% of the time in connected speech	Example words
/l/	*l*	75	*lamp*
	ll	18	*follow*
	le	8	*castle*

Approximants

Approximants are like the lateral /l/, in that air escapes without frication. However, the airflow is central. There are three approximants in English. They are all voiced.

The sound /r/ is a voiced post-alveolar approximant. The tongue tip curls back slightly, so that it lies opposite the back of the alveolar region and front of the palatal region, without causing frication. The vocal cords are vibrating.

The sound /w/ is a voiced labio-velar approximant. Two things are happening: the lips round into a circle, and the back of the tongue moves towards the velum. Neither involves frication. Hence the two-part term *labio-velar*. The vocal cords are vibrating.

The sound /j/ is a voiced palatal approximant. The tongue front moves towards the hard palate, without causing frication. The vocal cords are vibrating. Carney (1994:254) gives three possible correspondences, but without frequencies, because '/j/ is not easy to deal with as a unit of spelling correspondence'.

Phoneme	Spelling	% of the time in connected speech	Example words
/r/	*r*	94	*real*
	rr	4	*carry*
	others	2	
/w/	*w*	64	*well*
	qu (= /kw/)	27	*quick*
	wh	5	*wheel*
	u	4	*language*
	others	<1	
/j/	*y*	19	*yet*
	as part of /juː/		*use*
	reduction of an underlying /iː, ɪ/		*behaviour*

In general, the symbols for consonant sounds are easy to learn and remember, because they have mnemonic value. Eight, however, are unfamiliar symbols and need to be learnt:

- /θ/ as in *think* /θɪŋk/, *nothing* /nʌθɪŋ/, *earth* /ɜːθ/, *bath* /bɑːθ/.
- /ð/ as in *this* /ðɪs/, *there* /ðeə/, *weather* /weðə/, *smooth* /smuːð/. Many English grammatical function words begin with /ð/: articles like *the, this* and *that*, and pronouns like *they* and *them*.
- /ʃ/ as in *shop* /ʃɒp/, *sugar* /ʃʊgə/, *passion* /pæʃən/, *fish* /fɪʃ/.
- /ʒ/ as in *decision* /dɪsɪʒən/, *seizure* /siːʒə/, *measure* /meʒə/, *occasion* /əkeɪʒən/. This consonant only occurs in the middle of English words.

Some words of obvious French origin may begin or end with this sound, such as *genre, barrage, beige, cortege, prestige*. However, many speakers use /dʒ/ in these words.

- /tʃ/ as in *chest* /tʃest/, *match* /mætʃ/, *question* /kwestʃən/, *cello* /tʃeləʊ/.
- /dʒ/ as in *jump* /dʒʌmp/, *badge* /bædʒ/, *injure* /ɪndʒə/, *fragile* /frædʒaɪl/. Notice that /tʃ, dʒ/ are the only consonant symbols involving two symbols. This represents the fact that the sound starts with a complete closure (the /t-, d-/ part of the symbols) followed by a fricative release (the /-ʃ, -ʒ/ part of the symbols). However, /tʃ, dʒ/ each count as one sound (phoneme) in the consonant system of English.
- /ŋ/ as in *string* /strɪŋ/, *conquer* /kɒŋkə/, *anxiety* /æŋzaɪəti/, *bank* /bæŋk/.
- /j/ as in *yacht* /jɒt/, *cute* /kjuːt/, *canyon* /kænjən/, *saviour* /seɪvjə/. You may wonder why /y/ is not used as a more mnemonic symbol for this sound. There are two answers: Firstly, these symbols are used not only for English sounds, but also for the same sounds as they occur in other languages. In Northern European languages (German, Scandinavian languages), the /j/ sound is regularly represented by the letter *j* in the spelling. Secondly, the symbol /y/ is used for a high front rounded vowel found in Chinese, French, German and Finnish (see the Finnish letter-to-sound correspondence list on page 33) – but not in English.

? Task 1.1 Searching for sound types

A Circle the words that begin with a plosive sound.

blossom	*Christmas*	*gnaw*	*phonetics*	*quick*
business	*counter*	*grocer*	*playground*	*tackle*
chalet	*distinct*	GMT	*pneumatic*	*therapeutic*
chase	*dressmaker*	*kiss*	*pterodactyl*	*thyme*
chasm	*gentleman*	*penknife*	*quiche*	*twenty*

B Circle the words that end with a plosive sound.

arch	*board*	*jump*	*monarch*	*scratched*
arctic	*bribe*	*kerb*	*rebuke*	*shirt*
aside	*debate*	*limb*	*restaurant*	*sleep*
ballet	GMT	*look*	*returned*	*string*
big	*invent*	*marriage*	*rope*	*trick*

C Circle the words that begin with a fricative sound.

cello	*fuss*	*honour*	*sugar*	*Thomas*
chic	*genre*	*philosophy*	*Susan*	*very*
chick	H_2O	*SOB*	*there*	*VIP*
FM	*hippo*	*sheep*	*thick*	*zinc*

D Circle the words that end with a fricative sound.

barrage	*eggs*	*jazz*	*Paris*	*rocks*
breathe	*fish*	*laissez (-faire)*	*path*	*save*
chase	*fox*	*lease*	*please*	*size*
chassis	*giraffe*	*loch*	*quartz*	*triumph*
cheetah	*grand prix*	*of*	*quiche*	*watch*
cough	*is*	*off*	*race*	*with*

E Circle the words that begin with a nasal sound.

gnome	*mimic*	*Mr*	*NASA*	*NEC*
knowledge	*mnemonic*	*MTV*	*naughty*	*pneumonia*

F Circle the words that end with any consonant sound.

banquet	*deny*	*garage*	*parquet*	*square*
debris	*draw*	*happy*	*pillow*	*stranger*
complete	*four*	*panache*	*rendezvous*	*thumb*

Task 1.2 Searching for /j/ words (page 10)

You are the frog on the shore at the bottom of the page. Make your way to the shore at the top by hopping only onto those stepping stones with words containing the /j/ consonant. You can only hop onto adjacent stones, but you can hop backwards if necessary.

Task 1.3 Searching for /g/ words (page 11)

You are flying the plane at the bottom of the page. Make your way to the airport at the top by flying through those clouds with words containing the /g/ consonant. You can only fly through adjacent clouds, but you can fly backwards if necessary.

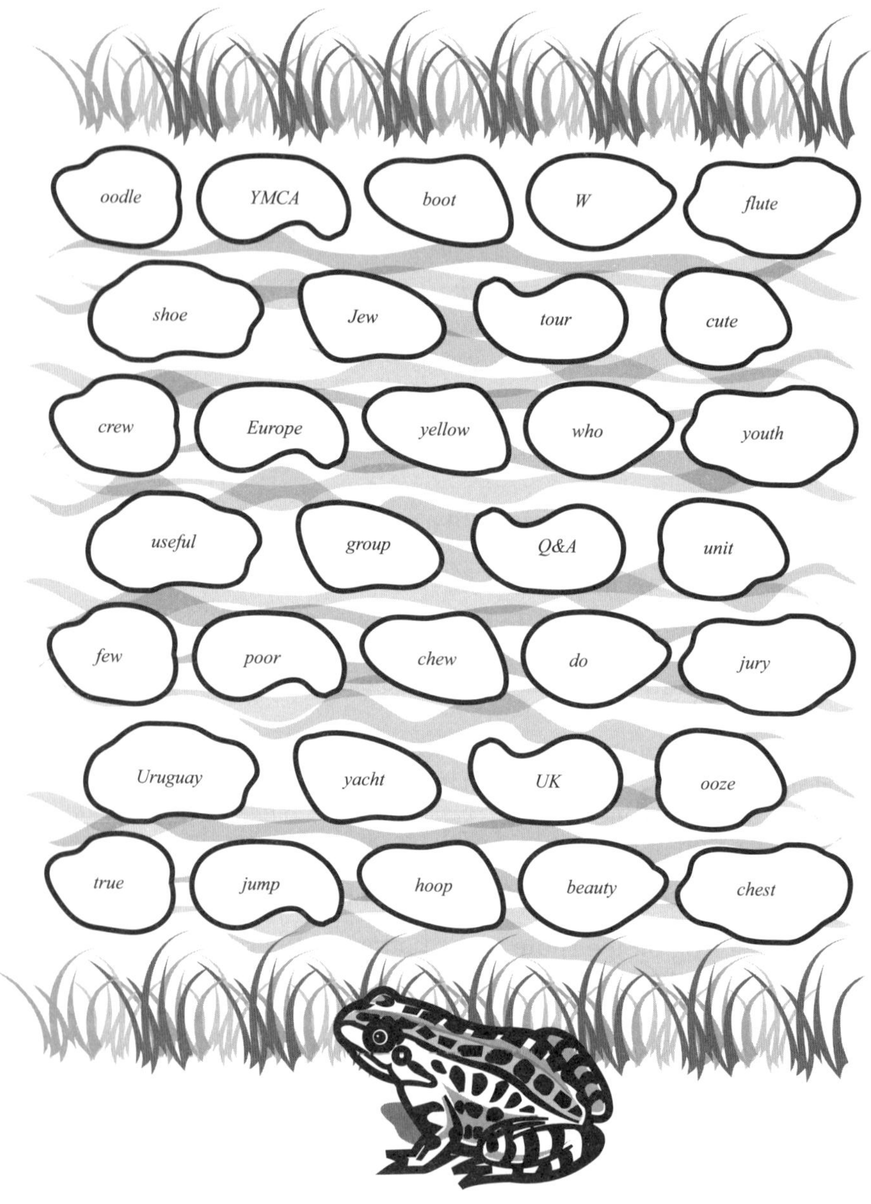
oodle
YMCA
boot
W
flute
shoe
Jew
tour
cute
crew
Europe
yellow
who
youth
useful
group
Q&A
unit
few
poor
chew
do
jury
Uruguay
yacht
UK
ooze
true
jump
hoop
beauty
chest

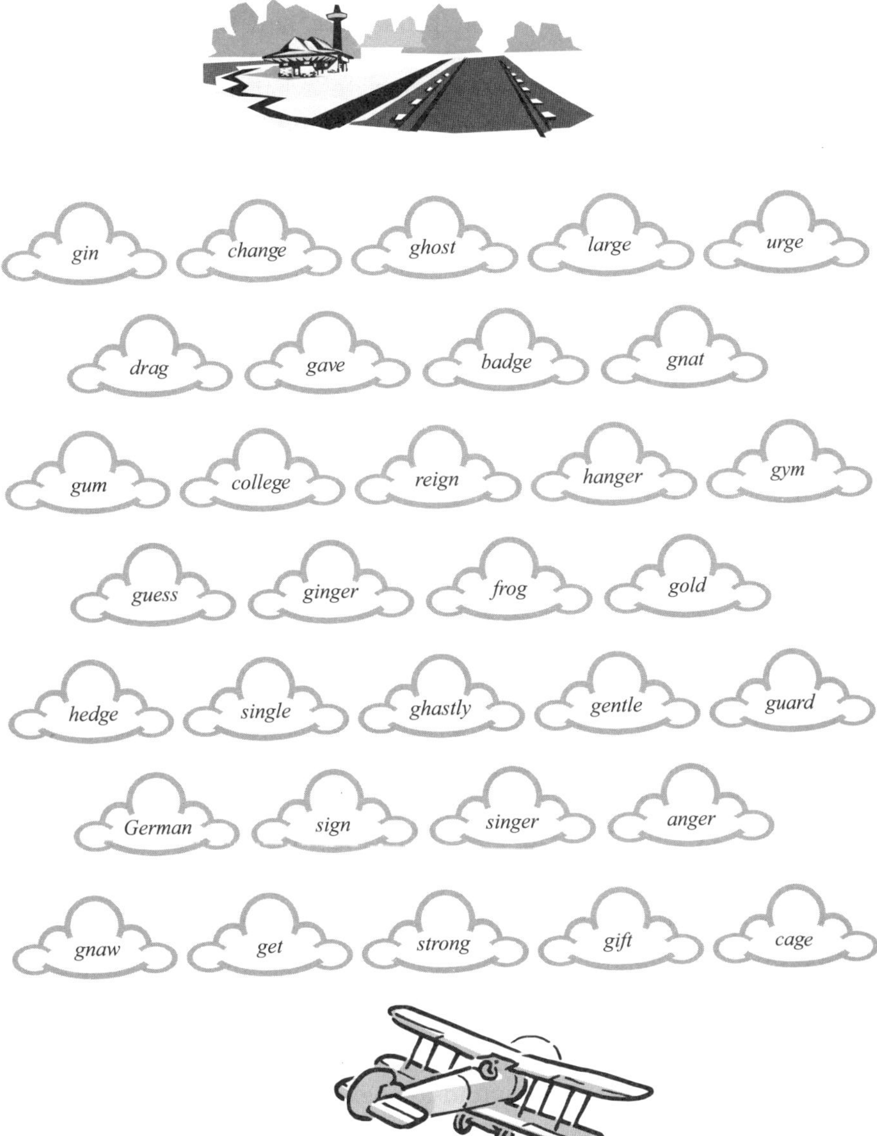
gin
change
ghost
large
urge
drag
gave
badge
gnat
gum
college
reign
hanger
gym
guess
ginger
frog
gold
hedge
single
ghastly
gentle
guard
German
sign
singer
anger
gnaw
get
strong
gift
cage

Vowels

There are 20 vowel sounds in British English. I have postponed description of these sounds, their production and their symbols until after the discussion on consonants for several reasons: Firstly, it is generally easier for readers to appreciate what their vocal organs (tongue, lips, etc) are doing for consonants than for vowels, since vowel sounds do not involve contact, but rather the tongue adopts a position in the mouth cavity. Secondly, the symbols for vowel sounds have less mnemonic value than those for consonant sounds. Lastly, the sound-to-spelling correspondences are less regular for vowel sounds.

English vowel sounds, all of which are voiced, can be classified in at least five ways:

- ***Monophthong versus diphthong***: Monophthongs are vowel sounds where there is no change in quality during the sound. For instance, the /ɑː/ vowel sound as in *bar* is the same at the beginning as at the end. In contrast, the /aʊ/ vowel as in *cow* starts with one quality and ends with a different quality. This change in quality may result from a change in the tongue position or in the lip position or both.
- ***Long versus short***: Long vowels are longer than short vowels. Diphthongs are long.
- ***Rounded versus unrounded***: The lips may be rounded or not.
- ***High – mid – low***: The tongue position may vary in the vertical dimension. This is usually obvious from the position of the jaw and chin, to which the tongue is connected.
- ***Front – central – back***: The tongue position may vary in the horizontal dimension.

It is not my purpose in this book to describe the articulation of vowel sounds in close detail (see the chapter Further reading and websites for titles that contain such detailed descriptions).

As for consonants, what follows is a list of the symbols for the 20 vowel sounds, each with a brief description of how the sound is produced, and of the main sound-to-spelling correspondences (from Carney, 1994).

Short monophthongs

The schwa vowel /ə/, which is a short monophthong, is intimately associated with stress placement. We will therefore not deal with it here, but rather in Chapter 5 on stress. There are thus six short monophthongs in English that we will describe here.

The sound /ɪ/ is a high front, unrounded, short, monophthong vowel, while /e/ is a mid front, unrounded, short, monophthong vowel and /æ/ is a low front, unrounded, short, monophthong vowel. The sound /ʌ/ is a low central, unrounded, short, monophthong vowel. The main sound-to-spelling correspondences for the short, unrounded monophthongs are given below.

Phoneme	Spelling	% of the time in connected speech	Example words
/ɪ/	*i*	61	*bit*
	y	20	*rhythm*
	e	16	*become*
	a, aCe	2	*spinach, image*
	others	2	
/e/	*e*	84	*ten*
	ea	6	*dead*
	others	9	
/æ/	*a*	100	*bad*
/ʌ/	*u*	63	*mud*
	o	27	*ton*
	ou	8	*touch*
	others	2	

The two rounded sounds are /ɒ/, which is a low back, rounded, short, monophthong vowel and /ʊ/, a high back, rounded, short, monophthong vowel. Their main sound-to-spelling correspondences are given below.

Phoneme	Spelling	% of the time in connected speech	Example words
/ɒ/	*o*	92	*not*
	a	6	*wash*
	others	2	
/ʊ/	*oo*	64	*good*
	u	32	*put*
	others	4	

Long monophthongs

There are five long monophthong vowels in English. The length is shown by the colon that is part of the symbol.

The sound /iː/ is a high front, unrounded, long, monophthong vowel.

Phoneme	Spelling	% of the time in connected speech	Example words
/iː/	*e, eCe,* final *ee*	38	*be, theme, agree*
	non-final *ee*	26	*deep*
	ea	25	*leaf*
	non-final *ie*	5	*chief*
	i, iCe, final *ie*	2	*motif, police, laddie*
	others	4	

There are three monophthongs that are produced with a back tongue position. The first, /ɑː/, is a low back, unrounded, long, monophthong vowel, while /ɔː/ is a mid back, rounded, long, monophthong vowel and /uː/ is a high back, rounded, long, monophthong vowel. Their main sound-to-spelling correspondences are given below.

Phoneme	Spelling	% of the time in connected speech	Example words
/ɑː/	*ar*	60	*park*
	a	34	*father*
	others	6	
/ɔː/	*a* (+ *l*)	29	*halt*
	or, ore, ar	25	*cord, core, war*
	au	9	*author*
	aw	9	*jaw*
	our	8	*court*
	ough	6	*ought*
	al ('empty' *l*)	5	*talk*
	others	9	
/uː/	*oo*	39	*moon*
	u, uCe, ue	27	*flu, rule, blue*
	o, oCe, oe	15	*who, move, shoe*
	ew	9	*new*
	ou	7	*group*
	others	3	

The sound /ɜː/ is a mid central, unrounded, long, monophthong vowel.

Phoneme	Spelling	% of the time in connected speech	Example words
/ɜː/	*er(r)*	39	*herb*
	ir(r)	18	*bird*
	ur(r)	15	*turn*
	or(r)	17	*word*
	ear	8	*heard*
	others	3	

Diphthongs

Diphthongs are vowels whose quality changes because of changes in the position of the tongue or lips or both. For this reason, their symbols consist of two parts, representing the beginning and end points. However, each two-part symbol represents a single vowel unit (phoneme).

Diphthongs are as long as the long monophthongs, for instance *buy* is as long as *bee*. However, a colon is not used to represent this, as it can be considered to be inherent in the two-part symbol.

There are eight diphthongs in English. These can be divided into three categories:

Diphthongs that end in a high front, unrounded position

Three diphthongs end in a high front, unrounded position. The second part of their symbol is thus /ɪ/.

The first, /eɪ/, moves from a mid front, unrounded position to a high front, unrounded position. The second sound, /aɪ/, moves from a low central, unrounded position to a high front, unrounded position. The third, /ɔɪ/, moves from a mid back, rounded position to a high front, unrounded position.

Phoneme	Spelling	% of the time in connected speech	Example words
/eɪ/	*a, aCe*	65	*labour, lake*
	final *ay*	18	*day*
	ai	12	*rail*
	others	5	

/aɪ/	*i*, *iCe*, final *ie*, final *y*	80	*bicycle, like, lie, try*
	igh	13	*high*
	non-final *y*	2	*rhyme*
	others	5	
/ɔɪ/	*oi*	61	*boil*
	oy	39	*boy*

Diphthongs that end in a high back, rounded position

Two diphthongs end in a high back, rounded position. The second part of their symbol is thus /ʊ/.

The first, /əʊ/, moves from a mid central, unrounded position to a high back, rounded position. The second, /aʊ/, moves from a low central, unrounded position to a high back, rounded position.

Phoneme	Spelling	% of the time in connected speech	Example words
/əʊ/	*o*, *oCe*, *oe*	75	*go, hope, toe*
	ow	18	*grow*
	oa	4	*coat*
	others	4	
/aʊ/	*ou*, final *ow*	93	*cloud, cow*
	pre-consonantal *ow*	6	*crowd*
	others	1	

Diphthongs that end in a mid central, unrounded position

Three diphthongs end in a mid central, unrounded position. The second part of their symbol is thus /ə/.

The diphthong /ɪə/ moves from a high front, unrounded position to a mid central, unrounded position. The second diphthong, /eə/, moves from a mid front, unrounded position to a mid central, unrounded position. The last diphthong, /ʊə/, moves from a high back, rounded position to a mid central, unrounded position.

Phoneme	Spelling	% of the time in connected speech	Example words
/ɪə/	*ear*	28	*dear*
	ea	12	*idea*
	er, ere	12	*hero, mere*
	ia	10	*media*
	eer	4	*deer*
	others	34 *	
/eə/	*ar, are*	59	*librarian, care*
	air	28	*hair*
	ear	10	*wear*
	others	3	
/ʊə/	*u* + /ə/ in suffix	†	*actual, fluent*
	u + /ə/ in stem	†	*cruel*
	oor	†	*poor*
	our	†	*tour*
	ure	†	*sure*

* As Carney (1994:190) says, '/ɪə/ is very divergent' in terms of sound-to-spelling correspondences.

† As Carney (1994:194) notes, many of these words are pronounced with /ɔː/ by many speakers. For this reason, he does not give percentages for /ʊə/.

It will be clear that the mnemonic value of vowel symbols is low and inconsistent, and therefore most of the symbols will have to be learnt to some extent. While it is safe to call /t/ 'the *t* sound', it is not safe, for example, to call /ɪə/ 'the *ear* sound'. The letter combination *ear* can represent /ɪə/, but can also represent /eə/ as in *bear*, /ɑː/ as in *heart*, and /ɜː/ as in *heard*.

Analytical problems

Triphthongs

Just as a diphthong is a vowel made up of two distinguishable parts (eg /ɪə/ starts like /ɪ/ and ends like /ə/), so there are some triphthongs that are potentially made up of three parts. Most writers recognise five possible triphthongs, all ending in a /ə/ quality:

/eɪə/ *layer*
/aɪə/ *fire*
/ɔɪə/ *royal*
/əʊə/ *lower*
/aʊə/ *shower*

A lot of variation is possible in the way different people pronounce these vowels. For many speakers, these do not have three distinguishable qualities. Instead the middle quality (/ɪ/ or /ʊ/) is omitted. The triphthongs may even be simplified into monophthongs. Thus, *tire* /taɪə/ and *tower* /taʊə/ may both be pronounced like *tar* /tɑː/. As a result, there is also disagreement as to whether these vowels should be considered to constitute one syllable or two (eg /aɪ/ + /ə/).

None of these theoretical problems need concern us, for the purposes of this book on phonemic transcription. In dictionaries, all these triphthongs are transcribed as given above, and any changes from a three-quality pronunciation may be considered natural features of connected speech.

/i/ and /u/

In stressed syllables, there is a clear difference between /iː/ and /ɪ/, as in *reed* and *rid*. However, this question becomes more complicated in unstressed syllables. In words such as *happy, react, hilarious,* do you feel the underlined vowel is /iː/ or /ɪ/? Some speakers identify it with /iː/, and others with /ɪ/. However, many speakers feel that it is neither /iː/ nor /ɪ/, but an indistinct vowel in that same general region. The vowel is always unstressed (as in the above words, and unstressed grammatical words like *he, be*), and therefore harder to identify (or perhaps it is less important to identify it). A solution commonly adopted by dictionaries nowadays is to use the symbol /i/ to represent either unstressed /iː/ (if that is how you feel you pronounce it), unstressed /ɪ/ (if that is how you feel you pronounce it), or an unstressed high front vowel that cannot be identified with either of the first two (if that is how you feel you pronounce it).

A similar solution is used for the unstressed high back vowel in *punctuation, virtuous* and unstressed grammatical words like *you, to* before vowels. The symbol /u/ is used for /uː/, /ʊ/, or something in between.

Syllabic /l, n/

In Chapter 6, we shall see that all syllables contain a vowel. The only common exceptions to this are words such as *people, vital, uncle, beaten* and *sudden*. All these words end in an /l, n/. The question is whether these final consonants are preceded by a short schwa vowel (/piːpəl, bi:tən/) or whether the preceding consonant is released straight into the /l, n/ (pi:pl, bi:tn/). In the latter case, which is perhaps the more common pronunciation in standard native accents, we analyse the /l, n/ as performing the same function as vowels usually perform, namely of being the obligatory central element in peak position of a syllable. They are therefore known as *syllabic* /l, n/. In order to accommodate those accents of English that have a /ə/ before the /l, n/, dictionaries often transcribe such words with the /ə/ in italics, or above the line, or some similar device, for example /pi:p^{ə}l, bi:t^{ə}n/.

In this book, we will use the full form (eg /pi:pəl, bi:tən/), with the proviso that the /ə/ is often omitted.

Task 1.4 Transcription to spelling 1

We are all used to reading words in spelling, and seldom give a second thought to the exact vowel and consonant sounds that make up the pronunciation of the words. In this task, you are given the pronunciation (in transcription), and have to supply the words in spelling. There are five of these tasks. This first one is relatively easy, with common words. The subsequent tasks contain progressively more difficult examples, in that they are either rarer words, or else the correspondence between the pronunciation and the spelling is less direct.

/hu:z/	/kəʊm/	/dʒu:s/	/jʌŋ/
/kɑ:m/	/ʃʌv/	/flʌd/	/lɪkə/
/def/	/det/	/temz/	/əkɜ:/
/eɪk/	/frend/	/ru:m/	/ɒnɔ/
/preə/	/brest/	/kʊd/	/prɪti/

Task 1.5 *Peter eats cheese in Greece*

The following exercise can be used with elementary learners, in order to practise the pronunciation of familiar vocabulary, and get them thinking in terms of sounds rather than spelling. It may also help them to appreciate how words they have read are pronounced.

1 Prepare a sheet with at least six categories: name, food, country, animal, sport, make of car, colour, film star, part of the body, etc.

2 The students can work individually, or in groups.

3 Give them a consonant or vowel sound, such as /f, aɪ/.

4 The students have to write down one example of a name that contains the sound (eg *Jeffrey*), a food (eg *fish*), etc.

5 Check that the answers given are correct, and award points. For a relatively easy sound, such as /f/, award one point per correct answer. For rarer sounds (eg /ʃ, aʊ/; see the frequency tables on pages 52 and 53), award two or three points per answer.

Here are some possible answers for /f, aɪ/. Can you fill in the rows for /g, ɒ/?

	Name	Food	Country	Sport	Car
/f/	*Jeffrey*	*fish*	*Philippines*	*golf*	*Ford*
/aɪ/	*Eileen*	*pie*	*Thailand*	*cycling*	*Chrysler*
/g/					
/ɒ/					

? Task 1.6 Transcription to spelling 2

In this second task, the words are slightly more difficult, in that they are slightly rarer words, or the correspondence between the pronunciation and the spelling is slightly less direct.

/haɪt/	/jɒt/	/breɪk/	/wɪmɪn/
/sɑːm/	/nəʊm/	/muːs/	/kʌbəd/
/wɪəd/	/guːl/	/fɪgə/	/resəl/
/næk/	/ɹaɪm/	/kʌzən/	/kɒləm/
/hɑːt/	/wiːz/	/bʊdə/	/plʌmə/

? Task 1.7 Searching for /e/ words (page 21)

You are the spider. Make your way to the centre of the web by passing through only those words containing the /e/ vowel (such as *web* and *centre* /web, sentə/).

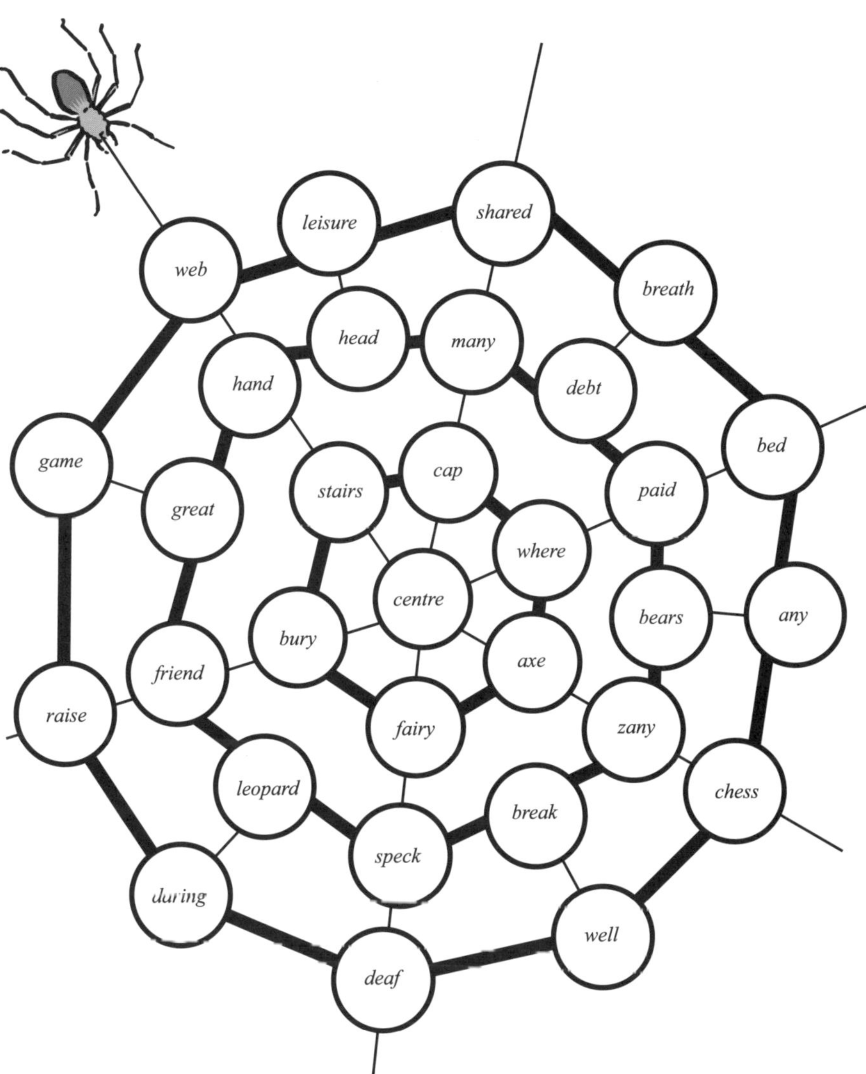
shared
leisure
web
breath
head
many
hand
debt
bed
game
stairs
cap
great
paid
where
centre
bears
any
bury
axe
friend
raise
fairy
zany
leopard
chess
break
speck
during
well
deaf

Task 1.8 Transcription to spelling 3

In this third task, the words are a little more difficult than in the previous task, in that they are slightly rarer words, slightly longer words, or the correspondence between the pronunciation and the spelling is slightly less direct.

/kreʃ/	/brəʊʃə/	/dʒɪndʒə/	/ləsuː/
/skeəs/	/dɪzaɪn/	/klʌmzi/	/bʊzəm/
/piːtsə/	/kənuː/	/buːkeɪ/	/rezəvwɑː/
/əkwɪt/	/kwɪziːn/	/sɪzəz/	/juːniːk/
/lækə/	/pænɪkt/	/flʌrɪʃ/	/sentʃəri/

Task 1.9 Searching for /ɑː/ words (page 23)

You are the dinosaur. Return to your nest by treading only in those adjacent footprints (horizontally or vertically, not diagonally) where the word contains the /ɑː/ vowel.

Task 1.10 Transcription to spelling 4

In this fourth task, the words are again a little more difficult than in previous tasks.

/saɪð/	/raɪð/	/ɪgzɔːst/	/vɪʃəs/
/wɔːls/	/sæʃeɪ/	/siːʒə/	/skwɒlɪd/
/sfɪŋks/	/sɒvrən/	/ʃæmpeɪn/	/repətwɑː/
/brəʊtʃ/	/saɪkəʊ/	/nɑːtsi/	/kɜːtəsi/
/skɜːdʒ/	/kliːʃeɪ/	/nɒlɪdʒ/	/nʌkəl/

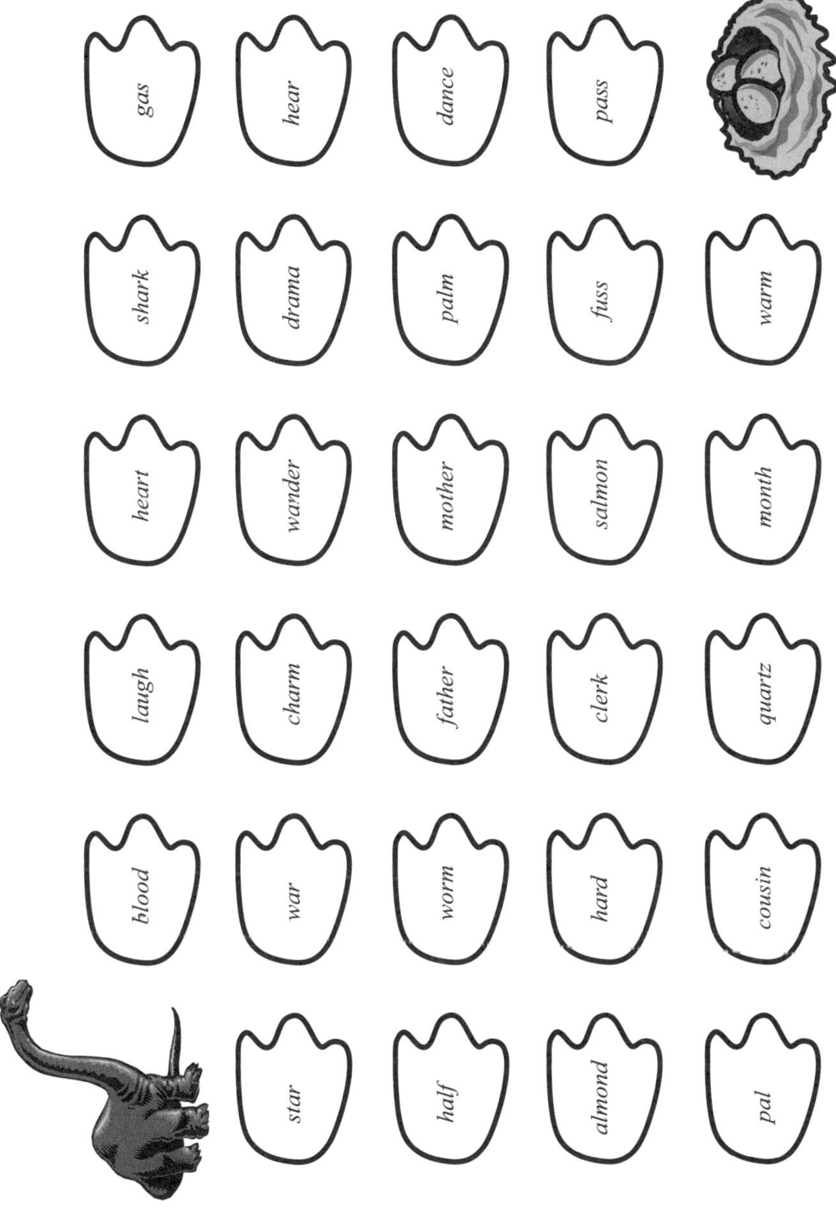
gas
hear
dance
pass
shark
drama
palm
fuss
warm
heart
wander
mother
salmon
month
laugh
charm
father
clerk
quartz
blood
war
worm
hard
cousin
star
half
almond
pal

Task 1.11 Sound anagrams

Anagrams are words that contain the same letters, but in a different order. For instance, *admirer* and *married* use the same seven letters. *Schoolmaster* and *the classroom* are anagrams. Some people use this to play games with people's names. Thus, *William Shakespeare* is *I am a weakish speller*. *The Reverend William Archibald Spooner* (see Task 6.8) gives *Reveal he'll mince both words read in pair* as well as *I, rascal Bill, improve 'red hen' to 'head wren'*. *Lewis Carroll: The Reverend Charles Dodgson* (see Task 4.4) produces *Oh, he's clever: records Wonderland girl's tale.*

This task is to do with anagrams, but, instead of jumbling the letters in the spelling, we are jumbling the (vowel and consonant) sounds in the pronunciation. Can you recognise the following names of cars, by rearranging their constituent sounds? For instance, the first one is *Rover* (/rəʊvə/).

ə v r əʊ	ə n d ɒ h
d ɔː f	ə s l əʊ t
əʊ v l v ɒ	əʊ r n e
ʃ ɔː p	z ə r k l aɪ
z ə d æ m	ə t əʊ t ɔɪ
ə p l əʊ	r eɪ l ə v e ʃ

Task 1.12 Transcription to spelling 5

In this final task, the words are either fairly rare, or fairly irregularly spelt.

/flem/	/tuːpeɪ/	/daɪəfræm/	/juːfɒrɪk/
/ʃætəʊ/	/zɪərɒks/	/ʃəʊfə/	/sɪluet/
/kɜːnəl/	/fjuːʃə/	/ətɜːni/	/kəmplekʃən/
/bjʊərəʊ/	/kæfiːn/	/prɒtəʒeɪ/	/beldʒən/
/tɜːkwɔɪz/	/nɒkʃəs/	/mɪljəneə/	/nuːgɑː/

Task 1.13 Identifying transcription errors

Each of the following transcriptions contains an error. Find the error and give the correct transcription.

Russia	/RʌʃƏ/	*maximum*	/mæxɪməm/
compare	/kəmpe/	*chief*	/tʃɪf/
ninth	/naɪnth/	*whisker*	/whɪskə/
quicksand	/quɪksænd/	*paragraph*	/pærəgrɑːph/
yesterday	/yestədeɪ/	*utensil*	/uːtensəl/
splash	/splæsh/	*Hannah*	/hænəh/
rainfall	/raɪnfɔːl/	*airport*	/eəpɒt/
custard	/cʌstəd/	*Finnish*	/fɪnnɪʃ/
anything	/æniθɪŋ/	*uncle*	/ʌnkəl/
javelin	/jævlɪn/	*Thailand*	/θaɪlænd/
archer	/ɑːchə/	*infer*	/ɪnfə/
fertile	/fɜːrtaɪl/	*homemade*	/həʊmeɪd/

Names of letters of the alphabet

Many people find it difficult in English to distinguish letters in the spelling from sounds in the pronunciation. There is a third difficulty that we must contend with – the fact that the letters of the alphabet have names. For each of the 26 letters of the alphabet, there are therefore three different aspects that we must consider:

- the written form of the letter
- the corresponding sound that the letter usually has
- the name given to the letter

Thus, for instance, the seventh letter of the alphabet is written as F (upper case) or f (lower case). It very regularly represents the sound /f/, as in *fall, if.* The name of the letter is pronounced /ef/, as in *I got an F grade.*

Task 1.14 Names of letters of the alphabet

Go through the 26 letters of the alphabet, and decide how the name of each one is pronounced. You will find that seven names contain the /e/ vowel (eg F /ef/), eight others the /iː/ vowel (eg B /biː/), four others /eɪ/, three others /uː/, and four others contain various other vowels.

/e/	/iː/	/eɪ/	/uː/	Others
F	B			

Task 1.15 Initialisms

The following sets of initials are made up of letters of the alphabet. They are pronounced as a series of letters (eg PVC /piː viː siː/), not as if they formed a word (eg AIDS 'acquired immune deficiency syndrome' /eɪdz/, not /eɪ aɪ diː es/). Some people reserve the term *acronym* for examples like AIDS, but call PVC an *initialism*.

Transcribe the pronunciation of the initialisms.

ATM (automated teller machine)
BMW (Bayerische Motoren Werke 'Bavarian Motor Works')
DVD (digital versatile disk)
HRD (human resources department)
ICBM (intercontinental ballistic missile)
LCD (liquid crystal display)
MSc (Master of Science)
OBE (Order of the British Empire)
POW (prisoner of war)
RSVP (French *répondez s'il vous plaît* 'please reply')
SUV (sports utility vehicle)
UFO (unidentified flying object)
VIP (very important person)
YMCA (Young Men's Christian Association)

Task 1.16 *A* or *an*?

A rule of English spelling/grammar that is often quoted in textbooks is '*An*, rather than *a*, occurs before *a, e, i, o* and *u*'. To test whether this is true, put the indefinite article in front of all the initialisms on page 26, eg *an ATM* /ən eɪ tiː em/. Which ones take *an*, and which *a*? Can you re-state the rule more strictly?

Task 1.17 Words that are names of letters of the alphabet

A common abbreviation in English is IOU. However, these are not the initials of longer words. Instead, they happen to be pronounced the same as (are homophones of) the words *I owe you*. The letters can therefore be used as a promissory note.

Consider the pronunciation of the names of the 26 letters of the alphabet. How many of them represent English words? For instance, the letter *I* is pronounced /aɪ/, which is also the pronunciation of the pronoun *I* (as in *I owe you*) and the word *eye* (as well as the rare word *aye*).

2

Background

We started in Chapter 1 by giving a brief description of the 24 consonant and 20 vowel sounds of British English, and their symbols. This was necessary because we need to refer to these sounds, their symbols and spellings in the rest of the book.

However, we now need to take a step backwards and ask important questions about underlying issues. Why do we need to pay much attention to pronunciation when so much English language teaching concentrates on written English? What sort of spelling system is used for English? Why does spelling seem to be so much more of a problem in English than other languages? How did the English spelling system come to be so bad? How can learners cope with the pronunciation of unfamiliar English words encountered when reading? Why is British English being used as the reference in this book? Is the system of symbols used in this book the International Phonetic Alphabet?

The priority of spoken language

We need to start in a fairly academic way by looking at the phenomenon called language. Here we are talking about language in general, as a system for communication that, for example, distinguishes humans from animals. Animals have systems for communicating with each other, but they lack certain properties that make human language far more sophisticated. Some people refer to this human faculty of communicating with each other as *Language* as an uncountable noun with a capital *L*, to distinguish it from particular *languages*, as a countable noun with a lower case *l*, such as English, Arabic, Swahili, Spanish, Mandarin.

This human faculty of Language, regardless of the particular language being used, can be manifested in different ways, or mediums. The two most common of these are the written and spoken mediums. There are other mediums, such as the tactile Braille system for blind people. Each of these mediums can be used for producing Language, and for receiving and understanding Language. We thus end up with the four skills familiar to English language teachers: writing, reading, speaking and listening.

	Written medium	Spoken medium
Production	Writing	Speaking
Reception	Reading	Listening

So far, the explanation has been simple and the distinctions should be quite obvious to all readers, especially teachers. However, one major focus of this book is the separation between the written medium (the left-hand column, with its letters in the spelling) and the spoken medium (the right-hand column, with its sounds in the pronunciation). As we will see, some people, including some language professionals, do not keep the two columns adequately distinct.

We now come to a fundamental question: Which is more basic – the written medium or the spoken medium? For many teachers and learners of English, the answer will probably be the written medium. One of the earliest English language teaching approaches – and one which persists even to this day in some contexts – was called grammar-translation, and consisted of translating written language from one language to another, with little attention paid to speech. Indeed, many people, including many teachers, believe that grammar only relates to writing, and that spoken language has no grammar. This is clearly nonsense, since in a language (whether written or spoken) that had no grammar, we could combine words in any order we liked. Spoken language has grammar (generalisations governing the way speakers combine words), just as written language has grammar. It is a different grammar, but it is grammar nonetheless.

Similarly, many tests written by English language teachers test written English, or involve written responses, far more extensively than spoken English. Many English language teachers take (written) literature as being the pinnacle of 'good' English.

If you ask learners of English how many letters there are in the alphabet, they will have no hesitation in answering 26. However, if you ask them how many sounds there are in spoken English, they will probably have no idea, and perhaps not even understand the question. (As we have seen, there are 44 sounds in standard spoken British English.) Everyone is understandably more conscious of letters in writing, as they are visible as marks on the page, or tangible as, for instance, keys on a keyboard or Scrabble tiles. However, few people without specialist training are consciously aware of sounds in pronunciation.

There are several countries where the emphasis in English language teaching is on reading and writing, at the expense of speaking and listening. Learners from such countries are therefore often very good in the written medium, but quite poor in the spoken. They find themselves at a disadvantage and flounder if they travel to English-speaking countries.

So, for most readers, the answer is probably that written language is more basic. However, if you read any introductory book on linguistics, you will see that it is the spoken medium of language that is considered the more basic. There are several reasons for this.

Firstly, from the ***historical*** perspective, every human society known to have existed has had the faculty of speech. Every society has therefore had a spoken language. However, not every society has had a written language. Over the course of human history, the majority of societies have been illiterate, that is, have not had written languages. Many languages did not have written forms until relatively recently (the last century or so), having been researched and given written forms by linguists.

From a ***biological*** point of view, humans seem to be innately predisposed to learning the spoken form of their native language(s). Many linguists, most notably the American Noam Chomsky, have claimed that humans have a language acquisition device (LAD), that is, they are pre-programmed to produce and recognise speech sounds. In contrast, not all humans have the ability to read and write their native language(s). This is obviously the case for speakers of languages that have no written form. It is also true of illiterate people, who, for whatever reasons, have never mastered the skill of reading and writing.

There are also differences in the way that proficiency in spoken language on the one hand and in written language on the other, is acquired. Humans without developmental problems start to speak their native language(s) at a very early age (say, onc year old) and have usually mastered all important elements of the spoken form by the time they start school at age five or six. However, humans start learning to write at a later age (perhaps at preschool) and, at least for English, continue to develop an ability in it for many more years. For instance, I only realised that the word *abbreviation* did not contain *-ie-* in the middle (in other words, is not spelt like *brief,* even though it is historically from the same origin) when I was studying at postgraduate level.

Also, the ways in which the spoken and written mediums are mastered differ. Children normally acquire speech by imitating the adults around them, principally their mother. However, they learn to read and write by being taught by schoolteachers and other adults. Learning to speak is a matter of subconscious acquisition, while learning to write is normally a matter of conscious instruction.

The ***functional*** priority of spoken language relates to what the two mediums are used for. Think of all the language you have produced today. How much of it has been in the spoken medium (speaking), and how much in the written (writing)? For most people, the answer is that they use spoken language far more often, and for more functions, than written.

Finally, there is ***structural*** priority. Let us illustrate this with an example. Can you write the following sequence of letters, as if they were a word of English: *gbftlh* ? Clearly, there is nothing stopping us from writing these, even though they do not correspond to a word of English. Now, can you pronounce the following sequence of sounds: /gbftlh/? You will probably have found it quite a mouthful! In other words, there are sequences of sounds that, for physiological reasons, are difficult or impossible to pronounce together. In short, restrictions on the combination of items exist in the spoken medium, but not in the written.

For all the above reasons, the spoken medium is considered in linguistics to have priority over the written. As a result, the overwhelming emphasis given to written language in some teaching circles is difficult to understand.

Although we have emphasised the priority of spoken language over written, this is not, of course, to say that written language is unimportant. The social prestige of writing is often higher than speech. For example, my name is written *Adam Brown* and pronounced /ædəm braʊn/. If I wanted to put on airs and start pronouncing it /eɪdəm brəʊn/ (with *Adam* starting like the word *aid*, and *Brown* rhyming with *grown*, both plausible pronunciations given the spelling), I could do so simply by pointing out to people that, however bizarre, that is how I want it pronounced. However, if I wanted to respell it *Addam Browne* (but continue to pronounce it the same, given that this is a plausible spelling for the pronunciation), I would have to pay a lawyer to make the change official by deed poll. In other words, spelling (the written medium) has legal implications in this case, whereas speech does not.

We have shown the two mediums as distinct columns, but there is the possibility of transferring language from one to the other. For instance, playscripts are written primarily in order to be read aloud. When dictating, we speak in order for someone else to write down what we say. However, there are some forms of communication which could only realistically be performed in one medium. For instance, timetables and telephone directories can only sensibly be written (printed), while warning somebody of an approaching lorry could only be done sensibly by shouting.

The alphabetic principle

Before embarking on the rest of this book, which attempts to familiarise readers with phonetic symbols used for representing pronunciation in dictionaries, it is important to take a look at some of the background issues that have led to the situation whereby such symbols are necessary. To do this, we need to look briefly at the alphabetic nature of English spelling, and historical factors that have affected it.

Writing systems

An alphabetic writing system is one in which the symbols (letters, graphemes) in the spelling represent the individual consonant and vowel sounds (phonemes) in the pronunciation. This is in contrast to the following systems.

Ancient systems

The early Minoans of Crete used a pictographic system, in which the graphemes (pictograms) are essentially pictures of the entities they represent; for example the meaning 'bird' was conveyed by a picture of a bird. Such a system might develop into an ideographic system (such as early Sumerian), in which originally pictographic graphemes became more stylised in shape and more conventional in meaning, for example a picture of a foot conveyed 'go, stand' and so on. A cuneiform system (as used in Assyrian) used wedge-shaped symbols, made with a stylus in clay, to compose originally pictographic symbols. The hieroglyph system of the ancient Egyptians, as with many other ancient systems, was a combination of systems: basically ideographic, but with some symbols representing consonant sounds, and others relating to the meaning of the intended word.

Current systems

The Chinese writing system, and the Japanese *kanji* system which is derived from it, are logographic systems, in which the symbols (characters) represent linguistic units (words) and often constituent parts of words (morphemes).

In the Japanese *kana* system, each symbol represents a whole syllable. In *kana*, the syllable is usually a consonant + vowel pair, although the symbols cannot be broken down into constituent consonant and vowel parts. Such systems are known as syllabaries.

The alphabetic principle

English, and many other European languages (such as French, German, Dutch), use what is known as the Roman alphabet. Other alphabetic systems include Greek, Russian, Arabic and Thai.

In a perfect alphabetic system, each grapheme would represent only one phoneme, and each phoneme would be represented by only one grapheme. This can be shown diagrammatically as follows.

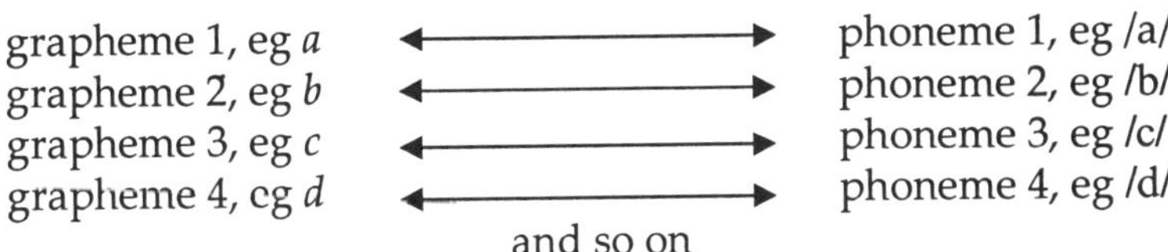

We say *would be* because there is no language in the world that is an example of a perfect alphabetic system, comprising a perfect one-to-one correspondence between letters and sounds. As we shall see, English is a very bad example of an alphabetic system. In fact it is probably the worst example of a fit between letters and sounds. Languages often quoted as having good alphabetic systems include Spanish, Finnish and Malay. To illustrate this, here are the letter-to-sound correspondences of Malay.

b	/b/	*k*	/k/ ([ʔ] syllable-finally)	*r*	/r/
c	/tʃ/	*l*	/l/	*s*	/s/
d	/d/	*m*	/m/	*sy*	/ʃ/
f	/f/	*n*	/n/	*t*	/t/
g	/g/	*ng*	/ŋ/	*w*	/w/
h	/h/	*ny*	/ɲ/	*y*	/j/
j	/dʒ/	*p*	/p/		
a	/a/ (/ə/ word-finally)	*e*	/e/ or /ə/	*oi*	/oi/
ai	/ai/	*i*	/i/	*u*	/u/
au	/au/	*o*	/o/		

You are probably not familiar with all the phonetic symbols used. Nevertheless the main point is clear: the correspondence between letters and sounds is almost one-to-one. The same is true of Finnish, although there are more correspondences to be stated, and the vowel sounds are more varied.

d	/d/	*l*	/l/	*p*	/p/
g	/g/	*m*	/m/	*r*	/r/
h	/h/	*n*	/n/	*s*	/s/
j	/j/	*ng*	/ŋ/	*t*	/t/
k	/k/	*nk*	/ŋk/	*v*	/v/
a	/a/	*ee*	/ɛ:/	*ö*	/œ/
aa	/a:/	*ei*	/ei/	*öö*	/œ:/
ai	/ai/	*i*	/i/	*öy*	/œy/
au	/au/	*ii*	/i:/	*u*	/u/
ä	/æ/	*o*	/o/	*uu*	/u:/
ää	/æ:/	*oo*	/o:/	*y*	/y/
äy	/æy/	*oi*	/oi/	*yy*	/y:/
e	/ɛ/	*ou*	/ou/	*yo*	/yə/

Again, the symbols may be unfamiliar, but the principle is clear: the correspondence between letters and sounds is nearly one-to-one.

What we have given above is the Malay and Finnish writing systems, in short, virtually everything that a learner needs to know in order to convert spelling to sound, and vice versa, in those languages. In contrast, what follows is the spelling-to-sound correspondences for the single English letter *c*.

In English, *c:*

- is sometimes pronounced /k/, eg *academy, balcony, romantic*
- is sometimes pronounced /s/, eg *cent, acid, excise, fancy*
- is sometimes part of the representation of /ʃ/ , eg *vicious, ocean, social*
- When part of *ck,* is sometimes redundant, being followed by the identical sounding *k,* eg *rock,* or is only required to avoid implications of a long preceding vowel, eg *package, hockey* (cf *hokey* /həʊki/)
- when part of *ck,* is occasionally 'silent', eg *blackguard, Cockburn* /blægəd, kəʊbɜ:n/
- is sometimes redundant being preceded by the identical sounding *s,* eg *science, muscle, luscious*

- is sometimes redundantly doubled, eg *account, accommodation* (cf *acoustic)*
- is sometimes not redundantly doubled, eg in *accident, vaccine;* the first *c* represents /k/ and the second /s/
- is /tʃ/ in Italian loanwords, eg *cello, concerto*
- as *cc* is /tʃ/ in Italian words, eg *cappuccino*
- when part of *ch* is usually /tʃ/, eg *chancellor, coach*
- when part of *ch* is /k/ in Greek loanwords, eg *Christmas, cholesterol, orchid, monarch*
- when part of *ch* is /ʃ/ in French loanwords, eg *charade, machine, panache*
- when part of *ch* is sometimes /dʒ/, eg *Norwich, spinach, sandwich*
- when part of *ch* is the velar fricative /x/ in some loanwords (if pronounced this way), eg *loch, Bach*
- is occasionally redundant, eg *acquit* (cf *aquatic), victuals, indict, yacht, Connecticut, blancmange, Tucson, czar*
- is sometimes in free variation, eg *defence ~ defense, disc ~ disk*

The list for the one English letter *c* is longer than the whole list for Malay or Finnish! Also, many of the correspondences (if they can be called that) depend on information that learners do not normally possess, for instance that *Christmas,* and so on come originally from Greek.

The history of English spelling

You may well be wondering why the English spelling system is so complex and irregular. The answer lies in the fact that it has a long history, and has been influenced in various ways during its history. What follows is a potted history of English spelling.

The Roman alphabet was brought to England by Christian missionaries in the sixth century. It soon supplanted the runic alphabet that had previously existed in England. The 23 letters of the (then) Roman alphabet were sufficient to represent the sounds of Latin. However, they had to be supplemented by additional symbols to cope with extra Anglo-Saxon sounds.

In the ninth and tenth centuries, parts of Britain were conquered by the Vikings, who brought with them their language (nowadays referred to as Old Norse), along with its spelling conventions.

Following the Norman Conquest of 1066, the newly arrived French scribes preferred to use the letter combinations and correspondences they were used to from French. By the 15th century, English spelling had become a mixture of French and Anglo-Saxon patterns.

In the 15th century, the printing press was invented, largely due to the work of Johannes Gutenberg in Germany. The first printer in England was William Caxton, who chose the accent of London as the standard to be represented in writing. Spellings thus came to be standardised, although, since many of the first printers in England in fact came from Europe, it was sometimes a continental standard of spelling correspondences, rather than a natively English one, that was used.

The next major event in the history of English spelling actually affected standard pronunciation rather than spelling as such. The Great Vowel Shift was a gradual process that affected the whole vowel system of English. Starting in the 15th century, it took at least a couple of centuries to be completed. Many vowels raised their tongue position, so that for instance, *goose* (originally pronounced with a vowel something like modern *dose)* came to be pronounced in its modern way, to rhyme with *recluse.* Similarly, its plural *geese* (originally pronounced something like modern *face)* changed to its modern pronunciation, to rhyme with *police.* Certain changes in consonant pronunciation accompanied the Great Vowel Shift. For example, the sound represented by *gh* in words like *bought* (something like the sound in the German name *Bach)* was dropped. The *k* and *g* originally pronounced at the beginning of words like *knight* and *gnaw* were also dropped.

The reason why these sound changes are important for the spelling of English is that, while the pronunciation changed, the spelling did not, because it had already been stabilised by the advent of the printing press. That is why modern spelling still has *o* and *e* letters in the spelling of *goose* and *geese,* where *u* and *i* letters might seem more appropriate. Similarly for consonants, modern spelling retains the (now 'silent') *gh, k* and *g* in *bought, knight, gnaw.* As Crystal (1995:274) points out, 'if printing had come a century later, or the Great Vowel Shift a century earlier, the present-day spelling system would be vastly more regular than it has turned out to be'.

From the 16th century onwards, some scholars felt that English spelling should reflect the historical origin of the word and, in this way, they increased the complexity of English spelling, largely by adding 'silent' letters. For instance, you may wonder why there is a *b* letter in *debt* and *doubt,* when there is no /b/ sound in the pronunciation, As shown in the historical Oxford English Dictionary, neither of these words has ever had a /b/ sound. Modern English *debt* comes from Middle English (roughly 11th to 16th century) *det* (alternatively spelt *dette),* which is from Old French *dete/dette.* Similarly, Modern English *doubt* is from

Middle English *duten/douten,* which is from Old French *duter/doter/douter.* The *b* letters were introduced by scholars because they knew that the French words came originally from Latin *debitum, dubitare.* The *b* letters, representing pronounced /b/ sounds, persist in Modern English words like *debit, indubitably.*

However, this attempt by scholars to regularise English spelling on historical grounds also produced errors. The word *delight,* whose *gh* letters were introduced by scholars at this time (in Middle English it was spelt *delit),* is not analogous to *light.* That is, it has never been pronounced with the /x/ sound that words like *light* had in Middle English.

Many of these false correspondences are obvious from the modern translation equivalents of these words: Modern French *doute, dette, delit;* Modern German *Licht.*

Over the last four centuries, colonisation has brought English speakers into contact with many languages around the world, from which words have been borrowed. Unfortunately, English has tended not to regularise the spelling of foreign words to make them conform to English spelling patterns. One counter-example is the word *snorkel,* from an original German word *Schnorchel.* However, many of the irregular spellings listed above *(cello, cappuccino, blancmange,* etc) are the result of not assimilating borrowed words to the spelling patterns of native English words.

Confusing letters with sounds

So letters of the alphabet in spelling must be kept distinct from sounds in the pronunciation in English. Unfortunately, many people do not maintain this distinction.

For ordinary speakers of the language, this is understandable: everyone is conscious of letters of the alphabet. They are one of the first things we learn as children (the A to Z). We can see them on the page, and we make conscious choices of letters when writing or typing. In contrast, sounds are ethereal. We simply open our mouths and out they come without much conscious thought on our part. We are seldom aware of what our tongue, lips, and so on are doing when we speak, or indeed of how many sounds we have uttered.

However, when teachers and writers fail to make the distinction between letters and sounds, it is a serious matter. These people need to understand well the way the language works. It forms the basis of their instruction, even if it need not surface explicitly in class.

As an illustration of how some English language professionals do not maintain the distinction, here are two quotations from published sources. To avoid embarrassment, I shall not quote the author or the book. The first is from a well-known Singaporean author, consonant clusters being a problem for some Singaporean speakers:

> We tried *latchstring* on our friends and they passed with flying colours. We believe this word with its six consonants in a row may be the largest consonant cluster in the English language.

The second is from a book for teachers written by a primary literacy coordinator.

> Consonants can be used singly or combined (blended) with other consonants. Up to three consonants can be used at the beginning of a word in English (as in *string, splash*) and up to five at the end (as in *twelfths*), although these words are rare. Investigation of three-consonant clusters at the beginnings of words will show that they all begin with /s/.
>
> *sch-* *school, scheme*
> *scr-* *scream, scramble*
> *shr-* *shred, shrimp*
> *spl-* *splash, splendid*
> *spr-* *spring, spray*
> *str-* *strong, stream*
> *scl-* *sclerosis* (not likely to be found by children)
> *squ-* *squirrel, squash* (although the third letter, *u* is not a consonant, *q* is always followed by *u* in English)

There are two basic errors in the above passages:

- The first writer does not take into account the fact that consonant clusters are combinations of two or more consonant sounds in either initial or final position within the same syllable (syllable structure is discussed in Chapter 6). *Latchstring*, being a compound noun composed of the two morphemes *latch* and *string*, is plainly also two syllables: /lætʃ + strɪŋ/. As a result, the *-tch* /tʃ/ is at the end of the first syllable, while the *str-* /str/ is at the beginning of the second. Since they are not within the same syllable, they cannot be considered a cluster.

Restrictions as to what consonants can and cannot occur together in a language can all be stated in terms of positions within the syllable. Any student who has mastered the /tʃ/ final consonant, and the /str/ initial cluster should have little problem in combining them into the sequence /tʃstr/ as in *latchstring*.

- Both writers confuse letters and sounds. There may be three consonant letters at the end of *latch*, but these represent only one consonant sound: /tʃ/ as in /lætʃ/. The ending of *latch* is no more difficult to pronounce than the ending of *attach* /ətætʃ/, even though the latter has only two consonant letters in its spelling. Obviously, spelling has nothing to do with difficulty here.

  Similarly, *twelfths* may have five consonant letters at the end, but these only represent four consonant sounds: /-lfθs/ as in /twelfθs/. The *th* letters represent only one sound: /θ/. It is not a /t/ sound followed by an /h/ sound. While this writer is clearly talking about letters when discussing *twelfths*, she is clearly talking about sounds when she says that three-consonant initial clusters 'all begin with /s/' (because she uses phoneme brackets).

  Although the list of words in the second passage all begin with three consonant letters, *sch-* and *shr-* are not the same as the others, as they represent clusters of only two consonant sounds: /sk-/ as in *school* /sku:l/, and /ʃr-/ as in *shred* /ʃred/. *School* cannot be considered more difficult to pronounce than *scoop* /sku:p/, even though *school* contains a 'silent' *h* letter, that is, it could just as sensibly be written *scool*. Likewise, the sound /ʃ/ represented by the letters *sh* as in *shred* cannot be considered simpler than the same sound represented by *sch* as in (a British pronunciation of) the word *schedule*, even though *sh* is two letters and *sch* three.

  The second writer also gets into a frightful muddle when talking about the word *squirrel*. In terms of sounds, there is no problem: the word begins with a /skw-/ three-consonant cluster, and may therefore be difficult for some learners (in addition to the /r/ and /l/ sounds later in the word). In terms of spelling, it is most reasonable to say that the *qu* letter sequence represents the /kw/ cluster of sounds, as it does in many other words, such as *queen, quick, square*. (Incidentally, there are words to be found in English dictionaries, where *q* is not followed by *u*, for instance *Qantas, Qatar, Iraq*. And there are many instances of *qu* which do not represent a /kw/ cluster, such as *quiche* /ki:ʃ/, *Qur'an* /kɔ:rɑ:n/, *unique* /ju:ni:k/.)

Designating some letters as consonant letters, and the others as vowel letters leads to unnecessary complications, as in the *u* letter of a *qu* letter sequence. The letter *y* is a consonant letter (representing a consonant sound) in words like *yellow, youth,* but a vowel letter (representing a vowel sound) in words like *rhyme, rhythm*. In short, it does not seem helpful to want to classify letters as consonants or vowels. In contrast, sounds can unambiguously be classified as vowel sounds or consonant sounds.

Strategies for finding the pronunciation of unfamiliar words

If you come across an unfamiliar word in writing, for instance when reading a newspaper, how can you find out the pronunciation of that word? As explained in the previous section, if we were speakers of Finnish, Spanish, Malay, or other languages with a close letter-to-sound correspondence, this problem would not arise. The pronunciation would be predictable from the spelling. But, because of the lack of a good correspondence between letters and sounds, we cannot do this for English.

There are three strategies we could adopt:

- Guess from the spelling
- Ask someone who knows
- Look the word up in a dictionary

Guess from the spelling

We could use the spelling of the English word as if it were a reliable representation of the pronunciation, and make an educated guess at the pronunciation. As we have seen, you will be right some of the time, but also wrong much of the time.

Many readers had problems when the Harry Potter books first came out, because Harry has a schoolfriend named Hermione Grainger. Since some readers had not heard the name *Hermione* before, and were encountering the word for the first time in writing when reading Harry Potter, they had no idea how it was pronounced. They thus resorted to several strategies:

- Some assumed it was a regular English name, conforming to regular English spelling-to-sound rules, as in the words *bone, cone, lone, phone, stone, tone, zone,* and therefore thought it was pronounced /hɜːmiəʊn/.

- Others thought it might pattern after the irregular English words *gone, scone, shone,* and therefore thought it was pronounced /hɜːmiɒn/.
- Others thought it might pattern after the irregular English word *done,* and therefore thought it was pronounced /hɜːmiʌn/.
- Others recognised the last three letters of the spelling as the number *one,* and therefore thought it was pronounced /hɜːmiwʌn/.
- Others thought it might be of Italian origin like *minestrone,* and therefore thought it was pronounced /hɜːmiəʊni/.

In fact, the middle part is pronounced on the pattern of *lion,* and thus the name is actually pronounced /həmaɪəni/. Note that the stress is on the second syllable, not the first.

This illustrates the problem with guessing the pronunciation of English words from the spelling – you are likely to be wrong much of the time.

Task 2.1 Guessing from spelling

Everyone knows that the *-ough-* spelling is a problem in English. Can you work out or guess the pronunciation of these (admittedly rare) English words?

brougham	'a one-horse carriage'
chough	'a bird of the crow family'
clough	'a valley or ravine'
doughty	'brave and capable'
hough	'a hind leg joint'
slough	(*noun*) 'muddy ground'
	(*verb*) (eg of a snake) 'to shed skin'
sough	'a murmuring sound, sigh'

Another big problem with English spelling is the existence of what are often referred to as silent letters. For instance, why is there an *e* letter in the spelling of the word *height*? The simple answer is that there is a letter *e* because there is a letter *e*! In short, there is no reason. Indeed, there are good reasons why there should not be an *e* letter in the word:

- All other common words ending in *-eight* are pronounced /eɪt/, for example *eight, weight, freight.* All other words containing *-eigh-* are pronounced with /eɪ/, for example *neighbour, sleigh, weigh.*

- The noun *height* comes from the adjective *high*, which we would not think of spelling *heigh*.
- If we were to spell *height* as *hight*, it would be analogous to all the other *-ight* words, that are pronounced /-aɪt/, such as *fight, light, night, sight*.
- The only counter-example that resembles *height* is the rare word *sleight* in the phrase *sleight of hand*.

So, the *e* letter in *height* can be called 'silent': it does not represent any sound, nor does it perform any function in the spelling. We could leave it out, and the remaining spelling (*hight*) would be a viable spelling for the pronunciation /haɪt/.

Carney (1994) distinguishes three different sorts of 'silent' letter:

- ***Auxiliary*** letters are an essential part of a complex spelling. That is, they may not represent an obvious pronunciation, but they cannot be omitted. For example, the letter *h* is often an auxiliary letter. In words like *shin*, the *h* has no obvious pronunciation of its own. Instead, it makes more sense to say that the complex spelling combination *sh* represents the /ʃ/ consonant sound. If we omit the *h* letter, we are left with *sin*, which is not a viable spelling for the pronunciation /ʃɪn/. Instead, it is now /sɪn/.

  Similarly, the so-called magic *e* at the end of a word like *shine* is an auxiliary letter. It cannot be left out, because *shin* cannot represent the pronunciation /ʃaɪn/. Instead, its function is to work with the preceding *i* letter to give the /aɪ/ vowel sound. The same is true of *hat, pet, rob* and *cut* (versus *hate, Pete, robe* and *cute*).
- ***Inert*** letters occur in underlying morphemes. That is, they do not serve any function in representing the pronunciation of a particular word. However, in morphologically related words, they may have a function. For instance, the *g* in *sign* does not have any obvious pronunciation. It does, however, have a function. Firstly, it cannot be omitted because the *g* is what distinguishes *sign* from *sin*. Secondly, there are related words like *signal, signature, signatory*, where the *g* letter does have an obvious function, namely of representing the /g/ consonant sound. In short, such letters are not pronounced (inert) in certain words, but are pronounced (active) in others.
- ***Empty*** letters have no function at all. If you remove the letter, there is still a viable spelling. The *e* of *height* may be considered empty. In fact, the term *empty* or *silent* may be too generous a term. Since these

letters have no sound and perform no function, but contribute greatly to the complexity of English spelling and the problems facing learners of the language (whether native children or foreign learners), they can equally be called *redundant* or *stupid*!

? Task 2.2 'Silent' letters 1

Take a sheet of paper and write out the 26 letters of the alphabet *a* to *z*. Then, against each one, try to think of an English word, in whose spelling that letter is 'silent'. For instance, for *a*, you could use *bread*, because the *a* represents no sound, and the word is pronounced the same as (is a homophone of) *bred*, showing that the *a* could be omitted. *Height* could be given as an example of the 'silent' use of the letter *e*.

? Task 2.3 'Silent' letters 2

For the following words, think about their pronunciation and that of related words, and decide whether the underlined letters are auxiliary, inert or empty.

autumn	*debt*	*hasten*	*phlegm*
bomb	*doubt*	*hate*	*receipt*
Christmas	*dumb*	*isle*	*shelf*
country	*give*	*lamb*	*two*

Ask someone who knows

The second method of arriving at the pronunciation of an unfamiliar English word encountered in writing is to ask someone who knows. This is a reliable method, provided such a person is available, and you can rely on them to give the right answer.

Neither of these will necessarily always be the case. In a school class, students can always ask the teacher. However, outside the classroom, the teacher or a comparably reliable or authoritative person may not always be available.

Secondly, the answer the person gives may not necessarily be correct, even though that person may themselves think that it is right. For instance, if you ask people for the pronunciation of *salmon*, many people around the world, including many teachers, will answer /sælmən/, as in *Salman Rushdie*. However, if you ask any British speaker, they will reply /sæmən/, to rhyme with *gammon*. In other words, the *l* letter in the spelling is 'silent' (empty). The pronunciation /sælmən/ is often known as a spelling pronunciation, the presumed pronunciation of a word given its spelling. As we have emphasised above, guessing from the spelling is reasonable for languages like Finnish, Spanish and Malay which have a good letter-to-sound correspondence, but not for English.

Look the word up in a dictionary

This is a 100% foolproof method, provided the word is in the dictionary you use, is not a rare or technical word, and you know how to interpret the information given in the transcriptions. This, of course, is the whole point of this book – to help you become familiar with the symbols used, and be able to work out from the symbols the pronunciation conveyed.

The other two methods described earlier are not 100% foolproof, for the reasons given. Whenever I am asked by a student for the pronunciation of a particular word, I usually do not tell them. Instead, I open a dictionary and show them the transcription. I do this, not because I do not know, or am unsure of, the pronunciation of the word, but because I want to emphasise to the student that they could have done the same thing themselves. In other words, I am emphasising the importance of becoming familiar with the symbols.

British English as a reference accent

The accents of English worldwide for which reasonably standardised transcription systems have been devised, may be divided into two main categories: those that pattern like British English, and those like American English. It is not feasible to write this book giving practice in the use of phonemic symbols, also taking into account both categories. The differences between the two phonological systems – and therefore their transcription systems – are too great.

The system used as the reference for this book is therefore British English, and the book may be used by anyone whose pronunciation follows the British pattern, or who uses a British model for pronunciation. Strevens (1980) devised a diagrammatic way of representing this, by superimposing a tree diagram over a map of the world (see Figure 2.1). The reference accent used in this book is therefore the right-hand branch in the diagram, and applies to:

- **Britain**: Most of England and Wales, but excluding Scotland and Ireland. Scottish and Irish accents are different in significant ways from those of England and Wales. Perhaps most noticeably, they are rhotic (pronounce /r/ sounds in words like *farmer*). This has a pervasive effect on the vowel system, leading them to require a different transcription system.

- **Australia**: While Irish and Scots did settle in Australia, they were outnumbered by the mid 19th century by the number of immigrants from England. Although the vowel and consonant phonemes may be pronounced in slightly different ways, they are corresponding phonemic units, and therefore the same transcription system can be used.
- **New Zealand**: While comparable numbers migrated to New Zealand from rhotic and non-rhotic areas of Britain, New Zealand English has turned out to be non-rhotic, apart from the southern end of the South Island, where the Scottish and Irish influence is strongest.
- **South Africa**: British settlers in South Africa came from different areas: those who went to the Cape came predominantly from London, while Natal migrants were from the English midlands and further north. South African English therefore shares characteristics with non-rhotic British speech, and the same phonemic transcription system can be used.
- **East Africa**: Large numbers of British emigrants settled in present-day Kenya, Tanzania, Uganda, Malawi, Zambia and Zimbabwe, and a British model was introduced in the education system.
- **West Africa**: In contrast, English was brought to West Africa by trade and several English-based pidgins and creoles arose, alongside the standard English of colonial officials.
- **The Indian subcontinent**: In 1600, the East India Company was established by a group of London merchants under a monopoly granted by Queen Elizabeth I. During the Raj, English was the official language of administration and education.
- **Southeast Asia**: Parts of Southeast Asia (Malaysia, Singapore) were administered as part of the British colonial empire by the East India Company.
- **Others**: Many other countries, for example in Europe, use British English as the model for pronunciation in English language teaching.

The above shows that British English, or a pronunciation based on British rather than American English, is widely used around the world in situations where it functions as a native, second or foreign language. British English is thus the reference accent used in this book.

Figure 2.1: Strevens' map-and-branch model of Englishes around the world (McArthur 1998:96)

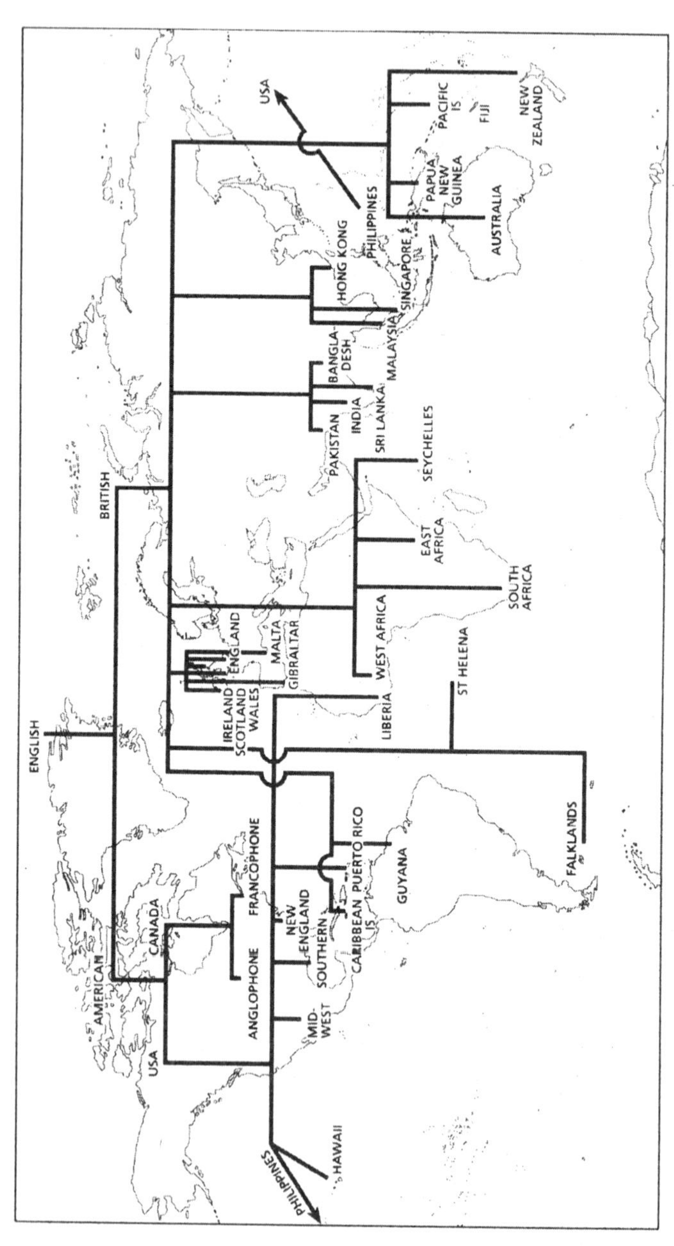

This is not to imply that American English is less important. Indeed, many writers have claimed that American English is more influential nowadays, due largely to the power of popular American culture.

'The IPA'

The transcriptions of English contained in dictionary entries are often referred to informally by teachers as 'IPA'. Strictly speaking, this is not accurate.

The International Phonetic Association was founded in 1886 in Paris by a small group of French language teachers under the leadership of Paul Passy. Their aims were nothing grander than to encourage the use of phonetic notation in schools to help children acquire realistic pronunciations of foreign languages and also to aid in teaching reading to young children. This is obvious from the original name of the association: *Dhi Fonètik Tîcerz' Asóciécon* (the *FTA*). In 1889, the name was changed to *L'Association Phonétique des Professeurs de Langues Vivantes* ('The Phonetic Association of Teachers of Living Languages', the *AP*), and, in 1897, to *L'Association Phonétique Internationale* (the *API*) – in English, the *International Phonetic Association* (the *IPA*).

> The aim of the International Phonetic Association is to promote the study of the science of phonetics and the various practical applications of that science. For both these it is desirable to have a consistent way of representing the sounds of language in written form. From its foundation in 1886 the Association has been concerned to develop a set of symbols which would be convenient to use, but comprehensive enough to cope with the wide variety of sounds found in the languages of the world; and to encourage the use of this notation as widely as possible among those concerned with language. The system is generally known as the International Phonetic Alphabet. Both the Association and its Alphabet are widely referred to by the abbreviation IPA.
>
> (*Handbook of the International Phonetic Association*, 1999:3)

Two important points should be noted:

- There is nothing specifically English about the IPA alphabet. It was created in order to devise a system for transcribing the sounds of speech which was independent of any particular language and applicable to all languages. Indeed, the *Handbook of the International*

Phonetic Association (1999) contains illustrations of the use of the IPA alphabet for transcribing 29 different languages.

- The IPA alphabet is phonetic, not phonemic. That is, it aims to allow people to transcribe human sounds, which is what the term *phonetic* refers to, in a strict sense. It does this independently of the particular language being spoken, and of the phonological status of the various sounds in the language. Sounds in a language group themselves into distinctive functional units known as *phonemes*. For instance, in the British English accent used as a reference in this book, there are 44 such distinctive units: 20 vowel phonemes and 24 consonant phonemes (see the list on page vii for these phonemes of English, and see Chapter 3 on minimal pairs for illustration of how they are distinctive). All true IPA transcriptions are therefore in phonetic square brackets ([ ]) rather than phonemic slant brackets (/ /). For instance, the IPA symbol for an aspirated voiceless bilabial plosive is [p^h], and for an unaspirated voiceless bilabial plosive [p], regardless of the fact that these sounds belong to the same phoneme in English, but to separate phonemes in other languages such as Thai.

In short, the transcriptions in this book are not IPA. The system of phoneme symbols used is that used with very little variation by reputable modern British dictionaries (as published by Cambridge, Chambers, Cobuild, Longman, Macmillan, Oxford). It was devised and popularised by A C Gimson (see Cruttenden, 2001). They will be referred to as phonemic (not phonetic) transcription in the rest of this book.

3

Minimal pairs

Definition

A minimal pair is a pair of words that differ in their pronunciation only in that the pronunciation of one word has one sound in a particular position, while the pronunciation of the other word has a different sound in the same position, the rest being the same. For instance, *chat* and *bat* /tʃæt, bæt/ are a minimal pair for the consonant sounds /tʃ/ and /b/. So are *catch* and *cab* /kætʃ, kæb/. We may also apply the concept to vowel sounds. Thus, *chat* and *cheat* /tʃæt, tʃiːt/ are a minimal pair for the vowel sounds /æ/ and /iː/.

Minimal pairs are important in that they show that the distinction between the two sounds is a critical one in the accent, because it keeps the pronunciation of words apart. The two sounds are thus basic building blocks in the sound system of the accent. These units are technically known as *phonemes*.

It is on the basis of minimal pairs that we arrive at the figure of 24 consonants and 20 vowels (phonemic units) for the British English accent being used as the reference in this book.

As is the case elsewhere in this book, the phenomenon being discussed here (minimal pairs) relates to pronunciation, which is what transcription represents. Spelling is irrelevant.

Task 3.1 Providing consonant minimal pairs

Provide one minimal pair for the following consonant permutations. Write it in spelling, and in transcription (it should be obvious from the transcription whether they are a minimal pair or not). The alternation may be at the beginning, middle or end of the word.

	/p/	/s/	/w/
/k/	*coke, cope* /kəʊk, kəʊp/		
/m/			
/tʃ/			

Task 3.2 Providing vowel minimal pairs

Provide one minimal pair for the following vowel permutations. Write it in spelling, and in transcription.

	/iː/	/uː/	/aʊ/
/æ/	*sat, seat* /sæt, siːt/		
/ɒ/			
/əʊ/			

Task 3.3 Identifying minimal pairs

Are the following pairs of words minimal pairs? If so, for which pair of sounds? (To help you decide this, you should transcribe the words.)

	Minimal pair? Yes/No	If Yes, for which sounds?
berth, birth	No	(Homophones – /bɜːθ/)
cedar, sadder	Yes	/iː, æ/ (/siːdə, sædə/)

You could follow the sample above when dealing with these pairs of words.

cell, Seoul	*ghost, host*	*phone, prone*
chef, shed	*grape, graph*	*sing, sink*
choirs, quires	*liquor, liver*	*though, trough*
dent, daren't	*mesh, mess*	*tomb, room*
fuchsias, futures	*model, muddle*	*wealth, Welsh*
germs, James	*peer, pier*	*which, witch*

Task 3.4 Frames for minimal pairs

The previous minimal pair task practised recognising whether two words given in spelling were minimal pairs, with a single difference in the pronunciation. This task gives you practice in the opposite direction, starting from the transcription (pronunciation) of potential minimal pairs and working out whether sequences of sounds correspond to existing words.

Here are five frames for you to insert vowel sounds into: /h __ d/, /b __ /, /f __ z/, /s __ t/, /p __ l/.

- Try to put each of the 19 vowel phonemes of British English (excluding /ə/) into each frame.
- Decide whether the resulting syllable corresponds to an existing one-syllable word of English. All the possible words in a column will be minimal pairs. For instance, the frame /h __ d/ gives you words like *heed, hid, head, had, ...*

You could draw a table like this for your answers.

	/h __ d/	/b __ /	/f __ z/	/s __ t/	/p __ l/
/iː/	*heed*				
/ɪ/	*hid*				
/e/	*head*				
/æ/	*had*				

Sounds and frequencies

If you open any elementary textbook on the sounds of British English pronunciation, it will list and describe the 20 vowel sounds and 24 consonant sounds. However, readers may be misled by this into thinking that the sounds are as equal as the teeth of a comb, that one sound has pretty much the same status and importance as any other sound. This is not the case. Among other factors, the frequencies with which sounds occur in connected speech differ greatly. In other words, some sounds are far more frequent – and may therefore be considered far more important – than some others.

The following tables give the relative frequencies of all the vowel and consonant sounds of English, expressed as percentages of occurrences of all sounds – both vowels and consonants (figures from Fry, 1947, quoted in Cruttenden, 2001:148, 216). The wide range in these frequencies is clear. This information is needed later in this book.

Table 3.1: Text frequencies (%) of vowels. Vowels make up 39.21% of all sounds in connected speech.

Sound	Frequency	Sound	Frequency
/ə/	10.74	/ɔː/	1.24
/ɪ/	8.33	/uː/	1.13
/e/	2.97	/ʊ/	0.86
/aɪ/	1.83	/ɑː/	0.79
/ʌ/	1.75	/aʊ/	0.61
/eɪ/	1.71	/ɜː/	0.52
/iː/	1.65	/eə/	0.34
/əʊ/	1.51	/ɪə/	0.21
/æ/	1.45	/ɔɪ/	0.14
/ɒ/	1.37	/ʊə/	0.06

Table 3.2: Text frequencies (%) of consonants. Consonants make up 60.79% of all sounds in connected speech.

Sound	Frequency	Sound	Frequency
/n/	7.58	/b/	1.97
/t/	6.42	/f/	1.79
/d/	5.14	/p/	1.78
/s/	4.81	/h/	1.46
/l/	3.66	/ŋ/	1.15
/ð/	3.56	/g/	1.05
/r/	3.51	/ʃ/	0.96
/m/	3.22	/j/	0.88
/k/	3.09	/dʒ/	0.60
/w/	2.81	/tʃ/	0.41
/z/	2.46	/θ/	0.37
/v/	2.00	/ʒ/	0.10

4

Homophones and homographs

We have already emphasised the fact that the English spelling system, despite being basically alphabetic, has a poor correspondence between letters in the spelling and sounds in the pronunciation. The correspondence, far from being one-to-one, is many-to-one and one-to-many. As a result, there exist in English many homophones and homographs.

Homophones

Homophones (from Greek *homo* 'same' and *phone* 'sound') are words that are pronounced the same, but spelt differently, such as /steə/ can be *stair* or *stare*. Some people take the opposite perspective, and refer to them as *heterographs* (*hetero* 'different' and *graph* 'spelling'). They are an inherent feature of the English spelling system, and one that is a problem for both native speakers and foreign learners, when writing. We can represent this diagrammatically as follows.

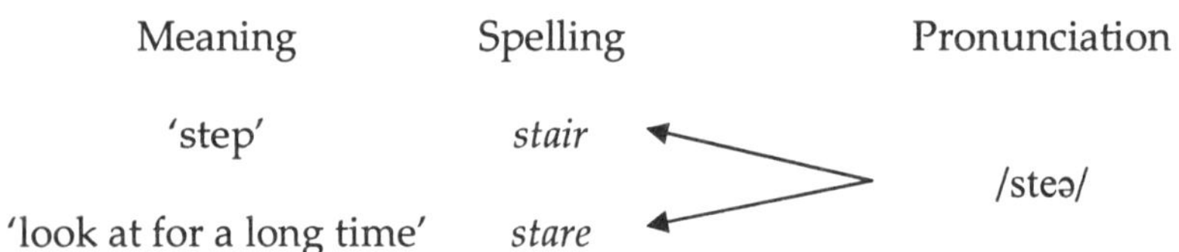

Because the two words are pronounced the same, they have the same transcription.

Task 4.1 Identifying homophones

Each of the following transcriptions represents a set of homophones. Write out the alternative spelling of the homophones, as in the first example. The number in brackets indicates how many homophones there are.

/steə/ (2) *stair, stare*
/kiː/ (2)
/dʒɪm/ (2)
/weɪst/ (2)
/ʃuːt/ (2)
/reks/ (2)
/grəʊn/ (2)
/siːlɪŋ/ (2)
/nəʊz/ (2)
/biːtəl/ (2)
/kjuː/ (3)
/sent/ (3)
/reɪn/ (3)
/waɪnd/ (3)
/preɪz/ (3)
/tʃek/ (3)
/maɪnə/ (3)
/weɪ/ (3)
/raɪt/ (4)
/siːz/ (4)
/mɑːk/ (4)
/piːk/ (4)

And the mother of all English homophones: /eə/ (6)

Homographs

Homographs (*homo* 'same' and *graph* 'writing') are the opposite of homophones. They are thus words that are spelt the same, but pronounced differently, for example *wind* can be said as /wɪnd/ ('current of air') or /waɪnd/ ('bend'). They can also be called *heterophones*. We can represent this diagrammatically as follows.

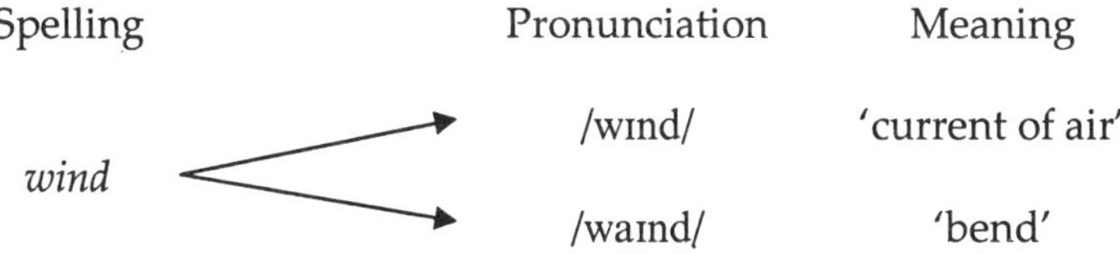

Because the words are pronounced differently, they have different transcriptions.

Task 4.2 Identifying homographs

Each of the following spellings represents a set of two homographs. Work out the two different pronunciations, and try to transcribe them using symbols, as in the first example. In each case, there are only two homographs: English does not have larger numbers of possibilities.

wind /wɪnd, waɪnd/	*sow*
bow	*routed*
live	*putting*
read	*aged*
wound	*minute*
use	*invalid*
tear	*entrance*
bass	*content*
close	*deserts*

Homonyms

To complete the picture, we should mention homonyms. These are examples like *bark* /bɑːk/ '1 sound made by a dog, 2 outer covering of a tree'. Here, we have two different words: we know that they are different words because they have different, and unconnected, meanings, and they have different historical origins ('bark of a tree' comes from Old Norse *börkr*, while 'bark of a dog' comes from Old Norse *berkja*). However, these two words have, over the centuries, come to have the same spelling and pronunciation in modern English. We can represent homonyms diagrammatically as follows.

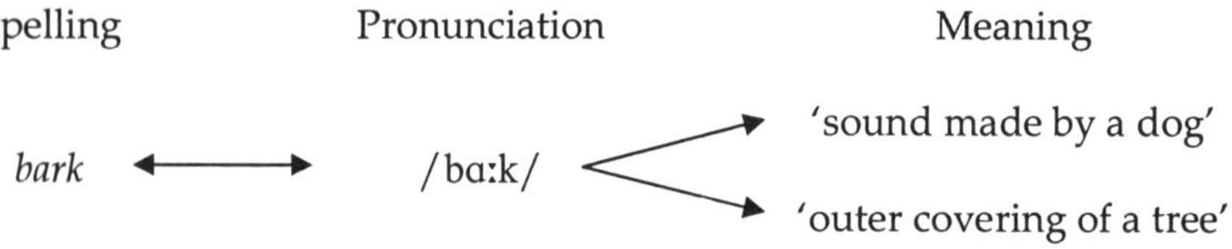

Notice that the divergence here relates to the meaning. It does not relate to the correspondence between spelling and pronunciation – hence the double-headed arrow in the above diagram, showing a one-to-one relationship between the spelling *bark* and the pronunciation /bɑːk/. As a result, homonyms may be found even in languages with good correspondences between letters and sounds, such as Malay.

Because homophones and homographs are an inherent aspect of the English spelling system, they are a problem for all learners of that system, whether native children or foreign learners. Many confusions persist into adulthood. For instance, many adults mistype *their* for *there* (and vice versa). Homonyms, on the other hand, since they represent a one-to-one relationship between spelling and pronunciation, pose no such problems.

Task 4.3 Identifying homophones and homonyms in jokes

Because homophones and homonyms are an easy way of making plays-on-words, they often appear in jokes and riddles.

In the following jokes:

- explain the joke, that is identify the word where the homophone/ homonym is
- either transcribe the word, or give its spelling

For example:
Did you hear the joke about the vegetarian cannibal? He only ate /swiːdz/.
Answer: /swiːdz/ is the transcription for both *Swedes* 'people from Sweden' and *swedes* 'turnip-like vegetables'.

Homophones

Why did the chicken cross the football pitch?
Because the referee shouted '/faʊl/!'

Why do we call the Middle Ages the Dark Ages?
Because they had so many /naɪts/.

A boy and an old man were standing in the aisle of a crowded bus. 'Pass /fɑːðə/ down the bus,' called the conductor.
'He's not my /fɑːðə/,' replied the boy. 'He's my grandfather.'

Have you heard the story about the Cornflakes and the Rice Krispies? I can only tell you it bit by bit – it's a /sɪəriəl/.

What pleasure does a monk have? Answer: /nʌn/

Two /raɪts/ don't make a wrong. They make an aeroplane.

Atheism is a non-/prɒfɪt/ organisation.

Not all the animals in Noah's Ark came in /peəz/. The maggots came in apples.

What's the difference between Noah's Ark and Joan of Arc?
Noah's Ark was made of wood. Joan of Arc was Maid of Orleans.

Homonyms

Time flies like an arrow.
Fruit flies like a banana.

I had to give up tap-dancing. I kept falling in the sink.

Policeman: Why have you parked your car here?
Motorist: Because the sign says "Fine for Parking".

How do you make a slow horse fast?
Don't give it anything to eat.

Patient: Will my measles be better by next week, doctor?
Doctor: Perhaps, perhaps not. I don't like to make rash promises.

Imagine you're at the top of a tower carrying a duck. How would you get down?
Pluck the duck.

Customer: Have you got half-inch nails?
Ironmonger: Yes, sir.
Customer: Then could you scratch my back. It's very itchy.

Customer: I'd like two lamb chops please, and make them lean.
Butcher: Certainly, madam, which way?

'Will you be paying in cash or by credit card?' asked the shopkeeper.
'Put it on my bill,' replied the duck.

The following schoolboy jokes are adapted from those quoted in Sue Townsend's (1984) *The Growing Pains of Adrian Mole*:

Q: What do you call a man with a seagull on his head? A: /klɪf/.
Q: What do you call a man with a shovel in his head? A: /dʌg/.
Q: What do you call a man with a very loud voice? A: /maɪk/.
Q: What do you call a man that can lift a car? A: /dʒæk/.
Q: What do you call a man that keeps stealing things? A: /rɒb/ or /nɪk/.
Q: What do you call a man who works out a lot? A: /dʒɪm/.
Q: What do you call a man with 50 rabbits down his throat? A: /wɒrən/.

And the biggest groan of all:

A Russian named Rudolph looked out of his window and told his wife, 'Look, it's started to rain.'

'That's not rain – it's hail,' replied his wife.

'No, it's *rain*,' insisted Rudolph.

'It's *hail*, I tell you,' retorted his wife.

'Look, Rudolph the Red knows rain, dear.'

Task 4.4 Identifying homophones and homonyms in Alice in Wonderland

Alice's Adventures in Wonderland and *Through the Looking Glass* were written in 1865 and 1872 by Lewis Carroll, the pen-name of Charles Dodgson (1832–1898). A mathematics lecturer at Oxford, he wrote many works on mathematics and logic, which appeared under his own name, as well as nonsense poems and books under his pen-name. The latter contain many examples of plays-on-words exploiting homophones and occasionally homonyms.

In each of the passages below from the Alice books, can you spot the play-on-words? Transcribe the word(s) that enables the play-on-words to be made.

'You promised to tell me your history, you know,' said Alice …

'Mine is a sad and long tale!' said the mouse, turning to Alice and sighing.

'It *is* a long tail, certainly,' said Alice, looking down with wonder at the Mouse's tail; 'but why do you call it sad?'

'When we were little,' the Mock Turtle went on at last, … 'we went to school in the sea. The master was an old Turtle – we used to call him Tortoise – '

'Why did you call him Tortoise, if he wasn't one?' Alice asked.

'We called him Tortoise because he taught us,' said the Mock Turtle angrily: 'really you are very dull!'

'And how many hours a day did you do lessons?' said Alice, in a hurry to change the subject.

'Ten hours the first day,' said the Mock Turtle; 'nine the next, and so on.'

'What a curious plan!' exclaimed Alice.

'That's the reason they're called lessons,' the Gryphon remarked; 'because they lessen from day to day.'

[A whiting is a kind of fish]

… said the Gryphon. 'Do you know why it's called a whiting?'

'I never thought about it,' said Alice. 'Why?'

'*It does the boots and shoes,*' the Gryphon replied very solemnly.

Alice was thoroughly puzzled. 'Does the boots and shoes!' she repeated in a wondering tone.

'Why, what are *your* shoes done with?' said the Gryphon. 'I mean, what makes them so shiny?'

Alice looked down at them, and considered a little before she gave her answer. 'They're done with blacking, I believe.'

'Boots and shoes under the sea,' the Gryphon went on in a deep voice, 'are done with whiting. Now you know.'

'And what are they made of?' Alice asked, in a tone of great curiosity.

'Soles and eels, of course,' the Gryphon replied rather impatiently: 'any shrimp could have told you that.'

There's the tree in the middle,' said the Rose: 'What else is it good for?'

'But what could it do, if any danger came?' Alice asked.

'It could bark,' said the Rose.

'It says "Bough-wough!"' cried a Daisy: 'that's why its branches are called boughs!'

Alice couldn't see who was sitting beyond the beetle, but a hoarse voice spoke next. 'Change engines – ' it said, and there it choked and was obliged to leave off.

'It sounds like a horse,' Alice thought to herself.

[Said Alice] 'If she [the governess] couldn't remember my name, she'd call me "Miss!" as the servants do.'

'Well, if she said "Miss," and didn't say anything more,' the Gnat remarked, 'of course you'd miss your lessons.'

[The Knight said] 'And then he took the helmet off again – but it took hours and hours to get me out. I was as fast as – as lightning, you know.'

'But that's a different type of fastness,' Alice objected.

[The Red Queen asked] 'How is bread made?'

'I know *that*!' Alice cried eagerly. 'You take some flour –'

'Where do you pick the flower?' the White Queen asked. 'In a garden, or in the hedges?'

'Well, it isn't *picked* at all,' Alice explained: 'it's *ground* –'

'How many acres of ground?' asked the White Queen.

Task 4.5 Searching for homophones 1

The following passage contains many homophones. However, the wrong homophone is given in spelling, for instance *weak* is written instead of *week*, both being pronounced /wiːk/. Can you:

- spot all the homophones
- give the correct spelling for the word intended in the context
- give the transcription (which is the same for both the wrong and the right word)

> Last weak, I took my deer, suite little dog to the beech. We went by our usual root, but along the rode, we had to break suddenly as their had been an accident. We sore a car being toad away.
>
> Having been borne and bread at the seaside, eye always enjoy these visits, especially on a sundae.
>
> My dog, Wrecks, loved it. I through a ball for him. Sometimes he court it; sometimes he mist it. Once he had to go into the see and swim against the currant to fetch a ball I had throne for hymn. I used to throw a peace of would, but he always Doug a whole in order to berry it.
>
> In the coarse of the afternoon, we went for a walk towards the navel dockyard father down the beach. Near the key, Wrecks started to weighed into the water and managed to fined some seaweed and muscles. He brought them to me proudly, and wagged his tale. But they smelt fowl, so I had to shoe him away. We won't go near that peer again.
>
> Later, I sat on the sand to watch the tied go out and the last raise of the son go down below the horizon. It was won of the most beautiful sites I've ever scene. But then it began to reign. Sew we got in the car and maid our weigh home as knight fell.

Task 4.6 Searching for homophones 2 (page 62)

Start at the entrance to the honeycomb at the top left of the page. Make your way to the exit of the honeycomb at the bottom right by moving from one cell to another adjacent one, where the two cells contain words that are homophones. For example, *bear* /beə/ is a homophone of *bare* (/beə/), not *beer* /bɪə/. Then, *ceiling* /siːlɪŋ/ is a homophone of *sealing* (/siːlɪŋ/), but not any of the other alternatives, and so on.

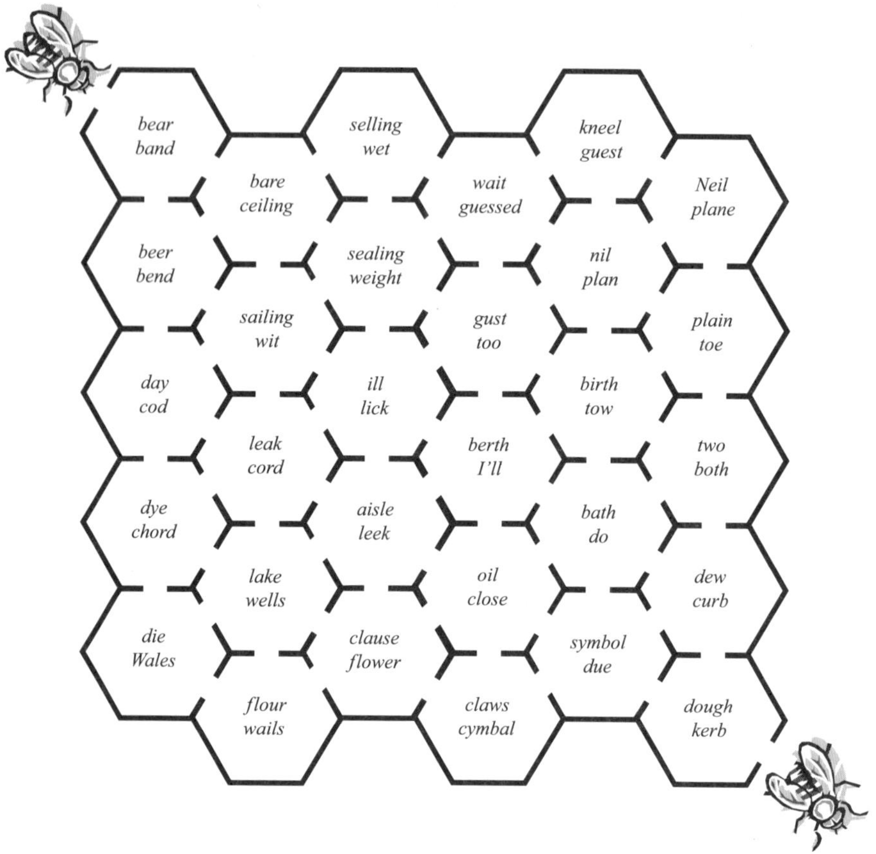
bear band
selling wet
kneel guest
bare ceiling
wait guessed
Neil plane
beer bend
sealing weight
nil plan
sailing wit
gust too
plain toe
day cod
ill lick
birth tow
leak cord
berth I'll
two both
dye chord
aisle leek
bath do
lake wells
oil close
dew curb
die Wales
clause flower
symbol due
flour wails
claws cymbal
dough kerb

5

Stress and schwa

In Chapter 1, we noted that the short vowel called schwa /ə/ is intimately associated with stress placement in words. For that reason, we only described six short monophthong vowels. In this chapter, we will explain the concept of word stress, and show how the occurrence of schwa relates to it.

Word stress

Words can be composed of one syllable (eg *cat, horse*), two syllables (eg *cheetah, baboon*), three syllables (eg *buffalo, gorilla, chimpanzee*), four syllables (eg *alligator, rhinoceros*), five syllables (eg *hippopotamus*), and so on. Where there is only one syllable in nouns like these, then that one must be stressed. Where there is more than one, English pronunciation tends to give stress to only one of them. The stress makes the syllable stand out from the others, and is produced by having greater loudness, greater length, a difference in pitch, and/or a full vowel, rather than schwa.

In the above words, the main stress could therefore be represented as follows:

CHEEtah, baBOON
BUFFalo, goRILLa, chimpanZEE
ALLigator, rhiNOCeros
hippoPOTamus

The placement of the stress thus becomes part of the overall sound shape of the word. Listeners understand what words are being said partly by virtue of the stress placement. The word *babble* (BABBle) is thus in fact very different from *baboon* (baBOON). Indeed, there are some words of English where the only difference in the pronunciation is the placement of stress, for example *insight* (INsight) versus *incite* (inCITE), *an import* (IMport) versus *to import* (imPORT).

How can we represent this graphically? We have just used capital letters for the stressed syllable, which seems to give the idea of prominence. There are various ways (or combinations of ways) this could be represented, for instance by a teacher in a classroom:

CHEEtah, baBOON (capital letters)
cheetah, baboon (underlining)
cheetah, ba**boon** (bold type)
cheetah, baboon (circle the stressed syllable)
chéetah, babóon (mark over stressed vowel)
Oo, oO (circles for stressed and unstressed syllables)

This is fine informally in a classroom, but something more formal needs to be used in the phonemic transcriptions in dictionaries. Most modern British English dictionaries use a tick above the line (superscript) at the beginning of the stressed syllable:

/'tʃiːtə, bə'buːn/

This tick may seem like a small mark, but it does a big job. The alternation between stressed and unstressed syllables plays a large part in forming the overall phonological shape of the word, in the same way as printing stressed syllables in capital letters does in writing. The tick shows where the stress falls, and conversely where the stress does not fall. You may have noticed from the above examples, that unstressed syllables tend to contain the schwa vowel.

The animals we mentioned above are therefore transcribed as follows:

/'kæt, 'hɔːs, 'tʃiːtə, bə'buːn, 'bʌfələʊ, gə'rɪlə, tʃɪmpæn'ziː, 'ælɪgeɪtə, raɪ'nɒsərəs, hɪpə'pɒtəməs/

Task 5.1 Stress marking

Which syllable is stressed in the following words?

absentee
assignment
cassette
computer
dictionary
essay

exam
grammar
pencil
phonetics
primary
register

revision
secondary
student
thesaurus
tutor
vocabulary

Task 5.2 Stress in *-ity* words

The suffix *-ity* can be added to all the following words (stems). Sometimes, this involves a slight change in the spelling or pronunciation or both of the stem, for example *generous* > *generosity*. For each word:

- pronounce the *-ity* version out loud
- decide which syllable carries the stress in the *-ity* word

Can you see any generalisation about where stress occurs?

available	*feminine*	*major*
Christian	*generous*	*national*
complex	*humid*	*personal*
confidential	*impossible*	*popular*
equal	*inferior*	*public*
extreme	*intense*	*real*

Task 5.3 Stress in *-ic* words 1

The suffix *-ic* can be added to all the following words (stems). Sometimes, this involves a slight change in the spelling or pronunciation or both of the stem, for example *drama* > *dramatic*. For each word:

- pronounce the *-ic* version out loud
- decide which syllable carries the stress in the *-ic* word

Can you see any generalisation about where stress occurs?

alcohol	*enthusiast*	*microscope*
algebra	*history*	*optimist*
alphabet	*idiot*	*organ*
angel	*Islam*	*photograph*
atmosphere	*magnet*	*syllable*
atom	*metal*	*titan*

Task 5.4 Stress in *-ic* words 2

The following words end in *-ic*, although not all of them can be considered a stem + *-ic*. Does the generalisation you just formulated work for all these words?

acoustic
Arabic
catholic
choleric
domestic
dramatic
Germanic
heretic
linguistic
lunatic
pragmatic
prolific
rhetoric
terrific
turmeric

Task 5.5 Stress in /-ʃən/ words

All the following words end in /-ʃən/. For each word:

- pronounce the word out loud
- decide which syllable carries the stress

Can you see any generalisation about where stress occurs?

acceleration
accommodation
Alsatian
coercion
compassion
comprehension
constitution
crustacean
cushion
Dalmatian
expulsion
fashion
generalisation
magician
mathematician
ocean
preposition
repercussion
representation
revolution
superstition
suspicion
tuition
Venetian

Secondary stress

With words of three or more syllables, we may find more than one syllable carrying stress. Let us take the five-syllable word *examination* as an example. As we have just seen in Task 5.5, the stress is on the syllable before /-ʃən/, thus /ɪgzæmɪˈneɪʃən/. However, you may have wondered whether all the other syllables in the word are unstressed. In particular, there seem to be two 'beats', one on the fourth syllable, but another on the second. The one on the fourth syllable is called primary stress, while that on the second is called secondary stress. There are several reasons for this: the second syllable carries some stress; for instance, it could be a beat in a poem; it does not carry as much stress as the fourth; it carries more stress than the first, third or last syllables; and the vowel in the second syllable is /æ/ and never becomes schwa. In other words, the second syllable seems to be intermediate between the fourth syllable, which carries the main stress, and the other syllables, which are unstressed. The same is true of the first syllable in *hippopotamus*. We could represent this thus:

eXAMiNAtion, HIPpoPOTamus

In phonemic transcription, primary stress is shown by a superscript tick, while secondary stress is shown by a tick below the line (subscript):

/ɪɡˌzæmɪ'neɪʃən, ˌhɪpə'pɒtəməs/

The schwa vowel

Although British pronunciation has 20 vowel phonemes, this does not mean that they are all equally useful. They have different text frequencies; that is, their rate of occurrence in connected speech. The most frequent of all the vowel phonemes is schwa /ə/. Cruttenden (2001, quoting figures from Fry, 1947) states that it accounts for 10.74% of all phonemes (see Chapter 3, Table 3.1). The reasons for this are that although schwa only occurs in unstressed syllables, it is very frequent in unstressed syllables; and unstressed syllables make up a sizeable proportion of all syllables. The next most frequent vowel phoneme is /ɪ/ (8.33%). The reasons for this are that it can occur in both stressed syllables (eg *bit* /bɪt/) and unstressed syllables (eg *orbit* /'ɔːbɪt/); and it is quite frequent in unstressed syllables.

Task 5.6 The schwa vowel

To illustrate this point, the names of several countries are given below. For each one:

- say the name of the country out loud
- decide which of the syllables is/are stressed
- decide which of the vowels in the unstressed syllables are schwa, and cross out their spelling

For instance, *Jordan* is pronounced /'dʒɔːdən/. You should therefore cross out the *a* letter in the spelling: J o r d ~~a~~ n.

J a p a n	G e r m a n y
K e n y a	G r e n a d a
F i n l a n d	L e b a n o n
Y e m e n	A r g e n t i n a
J a m a i c a	M a u r i t i u s
M o n a c o	V e n e z u e l a

Bermuda
Switzerland
The Bahamas
Canada
Morocco
The Netherlands
Guatemala
Costa Rica
The Solomon Islands
Western Samoa

Task 5.7 Word-final schwa

One problem with the schwa vowel /ə/ is that it does not have any standard spelling; that is, there is no letter that regularly represents schwa. In this exercise, we give you various spellings that can represent schwa in certain words. The schwa is the last sound in the word. Can you think of one example of each of the following possible spellings for final schwa? For instance *-er* is illustrated by *teacher* /tiːtʃə/.

-a
-ah
-ar
-e
-er
-eur
-ire
-or
-ough
-our
-re
-ur
-ure
-yr

Stress in grammatical words

Words do not occur in isolation, but in phrases, clauses, sentences and passages. But not all words do the same amount of work. Linguists divide words into two main categories. Lexical content words are the nouns, main verbs, adjectives and adverbs that carry most of the meaning. Grammatical function words are the other grammatical categories (articles, prepositions, auxiliary verbs, conjunctions, etc) that do not convey so much of the meaning. Grammatical function words need to be there in order to make grammatical sentences, but they do not add much to the meaning of the message.

Task 5.8 Providing grammatical function words

To show that this is the case, here is the first paragraph of a section in Chapter 2 of this book. However, this time, I have written it replacing all the grammatical function words with a blank. Can you work out what they are without referring to the paragraph on page 28?

_____ need _____ start _____ _____ fairly academic way _____ looking _____ _____ phenomenon called language. Here _____ _____ talking _____ language _____ general, _____ _____ system _____ communication _____ , _____ example, distinguishes humans _____ animals. Animals have systems _____ communicating _____ each other, _____ _____ lack certain properties _____ make human language far more sophisticated. Some people refer _____ this human faculty _____ communicating _____ each other _____ *Language* _____ _____ uncountable noun _____ _____ capital *L*, _____ distinguish _____ _____ particular *languages*, _____ _____ countable noun _____ _____ lower case *l*, such _____ English, Arabic, Swahili, Spanish, Mandarin.

Schwa in connected speech

To summarise, schwa is the most frequent of all the vowel phonemes. The reasons for this are that although schwa only occurs in unstressed syllables, it is very frequent in unstressed syllables; and unstressed syllables make up a sizeable proportion of all syllables. Schwa is common as the vowel in unstressed syllables of multi-syllable words, and in grammatical function words occurring in connected speech. This weak pronunciation is often represented in spelling, for example *rock 'n' roll*.

Here is the same passage as in the previous task. However, this time, I have printed it substituting the schwa symbol for any vowel letter that would normally be pronounced as schwa in connected speech. Read through the passage paying special attention to the occurrences of schwa. (Notice that I am, for the purposes of this task, mixing the schwa phonemic symbol with regular spelling.)

We need tə start in ə fairly acədemic way by looking ət thə phənomənən called language. Here we ə talking əbout language in gen(ə)rəl, əs ə systəm fər cəmmunicatən thət, fər exampəl, distinguishes huməns frəm animəls. Animəls have systəms fər cəmmunicating with each othər, bət they lack certən propərties thət make humən language far more səphisticated. Some peopəl refer tə this humən facəlty əf cəmmunicating with each othər əs *Language* əs ən uncountəbəl noun with ə capitəl *L*, tə distinguish it frəm pərticələr *languages*, əs ə countəbəl noun with ə lowər case *l*, such əs English, Arəbic, Swahili, Spanish, Mandərin.

6

Syllable structure

In the last chapter we saw that, in words with more than one syllable, one of those syllables stands out from the rest by being stressed. Stress placement within words is a major part of the overall phonological shape of the word, but is not often predictable in English. Therefore, it has to be shown in dictionary transcriptions.

In this chapter, we look at the internal composition of syllables. You may wonder why we need to do this. There are several reasons why the syllable is an important unit:

- As we have seen in Chapter 2, there are some languages that have writing systems based on the syllable, such as the Japanese *kana* syllabary system.
- Everyone, regardless of their native language and its writing system, seems to be able to identify how many syllables words contain. You probably have no difficulty or doubt in stating that *English* has two syllables, *language* two, and *department* three. But not everyone can state how many consonant and vowel segments are contained within those syllables.
- Differences between languages can be stated in terms of the syllable and its structure. That is, we can imagine two languages with identical consonant and vowel phonemic units, but which combine those segments in different ways to make syllables and words.
- These differences are likely to lead to difficulties for foreign learners in pronouncing certain English combinations, and in transcribing them correctly. And, vice versa, English speakers will have problems with sound combinations in foreign languages.
- Literacy experts are generally agreed that an awareness of the sounds that make up syllables, and of phenomena such as alliteration and rhyme, are essential for efficient spellers of English.

Parts of a syllable

Phonologists divide the syllable into three parts. You may have noticed that the word *English* not only has two syllables, but also two vowels /ɪ, ɪ/. Similarly, *language* has two syllables and two vowels /æ, ɪ/, and *department* three of each /ɪ, ɑː, ə/. The vowel is thus a central part of the syllable, and occupies the central position. In this book, we will refer to this position as the *peak,* although other writers use terms such as *nuclear, syllabic* and *syllable-medial* position. Preceding the vowel, there may be nothing. For instance, the first syllable of *English* /ɪŋ/ has nothing before the /ɪ/ vowel. However, there is often one or more consonants. For instance, the first syllable of *language* /læŋ/ has one initial consonant (/l/). So does every syllable in *department.* These initial consonants occupy what we will call *onset* position. Others call it *syllable-initial* or *releasing* position. Following the vowel, there may be nothing, as in the first syllable of *department* /dɪ/. Or there may be consonants, as in the other syllables. This position is known as *coda* (or *syllable-final,* or *arresting* position).

We may therefore analyse the syllables of the phrase *English language department* as follows:

Onset	Peak	Coda
	ɪ	ŋ
gl	ɪ	ʃ
l	æ	ŋ
gw	ɪ	ʤ
d	ɪ	
p	ɑː	t
m	ə	nt

Where there is more than one consonant phoneme in either onset or coda position, this is known as a consonant *cluster.* Thus, the second syllable of language /gwɪʤ/ has a two-consonant initial cluster /gw-/, and the final syllable of department /mənt/ has a two-consonant final cluster /-nt/. Remember that the symbols for the fricatives /ʧ, ʤ/ contain two symbols, but only represent one phonemic unit. The phoneme /ʤ/ at the end of *language* is therefore not a cluster.

Task 6.1 Analysing syllable structure

Transcribe the following monosyllabic words, and put the symbols in the correct column to show their syllable structure. (Hint: place the vowel symbol in peak first, and the consonant placements should be easy.) Then say which of the words contain consonant clusters.

	Onset	Peak	Coda	Cluster?
pin	p	ɪ	n	No
stripe	str	aɪ	p	Yes, initial /str/

two	*phoned*	*voiced*	*washed*
step	*sprint*	*write*	*eight*
sails	*mixed*	*through*	*yacht*
thank	*eye*	*schools*	*flex*
once	*quirk*	*twelfths*	*gnome*

English allows initial clusters of up to three consonants, as in *stripe* /straɪp/, and final clusters of up to four consonants, as in *twelfths* /twelfθs/. However, final clusters of more than two or three consonants are rare, and may be simplified in practice by deleting one or more of the consonants.

The formula $C_{0\text{-}3}\ V\ C_{0\text{-}4}$ can be used to represent English syllable structure, where C and V represent any consonant or vowel phoneme. In terms of languages worldwide, this is more complex than most. Other examples are (O represents no consonant, that is C_0):

Tswana*	$C_{0\text{-}1}$ V O	(ie only V and CV syllables)
Cantonese	$C_{0\text{-}1}$ V $C_{0\text{-}1}$	(ie no clusters)
Spanish	$C_{0\text{-}2}$ V $C_{0\text{-}1}$	(ie initial clusters but no final clusters)
Arabic	$C_{0\text{-}1}$ V $C_{0\text{-}2}$	(ie final clusters but no initial clusters)
Russian	$C_{0\text{-}4}$ V $C_{0\text{-}4}$	

* A language of Botswana

Alliteration

Two (or more) syllables are said to alliterate if they have the same onsets. It is a very common feature of poetry and other genres.

> Now the news. Night raids on
> Five cities. Fires started.
> Pressure applied by pincer movement
> In threatening thrust. Third Division
> Enlarges beachhead. Lucky charm
> Saves sniper. Sabotage hinted
> In steel-mill stoppage …
>
> (W H Auden *The Age of Anxiety*)

> Peter Piper picked a peck of pickled peppers.

> Round and round the rugged rock the ragged rascal ran.

> 'Step forward, Tin Man. You dare to come to me for a heart, do you? You clinking, clanking, clattering collection of caliginous junk … And you, Scarecrow, have the effrontery to ask for a brain! You billowing bale of bovine fodder!'
>
> (The Wizard of Oz, from the 1939 MGM film)

Did you notice the identical onset /n/s of *now, news, night*; the /f/s of *five, fires*; the /θr/s of *threatening, thrust*; the /l/s of *(en)larges, lucky*; the /s/s of *saves, sabotage*; and the /st/s of *steel, stoppage*? And there were several near-alliterations in that poem: /p/ is repeated in *pressure, (ap)plied, pincer,* /θ/ in *third,* /s/ in *sniper*.

Notice that spelling is irrelevant. Thus the saying *Curiosity killed the cat* alliterates, even though the initial /k/ sounds are spelt with either *c* or *k* letters.

Task 6.2 Alliteration in similes

A simile is when you compare one thing to something else, usually with the words *like* or *as*. In English, there are a number of common similes that employ alliteration and near-alliteration. Can you complete the following similes?

as busy as a /b/...	as large as /l/...
as dead as a /d/...	as bright as a /b/...
as proud as a /p/...	as mad as a /m/...

as fit as a /f/...
as bold as /b/...
as good as /g/...
as cool as a /k/...
as still as a /st/...
as pretty as a /p/...
as pleased as /p/...
as blind as a /b/...
as thick as /θ/...
as right as /r/...
as green as /gr/...
as plump as a /p/...

Task 6.3 Alliteration in fixed expressions

There are many other fixed expressions that rely on alliteration. Can you complete the following common expressions?

this and /ð/...
rough and /r/...
spick and /sp/...
hale and /h/...
jump for /dʒ/ ...
back to /b/ ..
beat about the /b/...
two peas in a /p/...
go against the /g/...
mind over /m/...
add fuel to the /f/...
not on your /n/...
put your money where your /m/... is
better safe than /s/...
through thick and /θ/...
part and /p/ ..
risk life and /l/ ...
without a /w/... in the /w/...
live in the /l/... of /l/...
tricks of the /tr/...
in dribs and /dr/...
His bark is worse than his /b/...
Where's there's a /w/..., there's a /w/...
It takes /t/ ... to /t/ ...

Rhyme

Rhyme is, in a sense, the opposite of alliteration. While alliteration relates to identity in the onset position of a syllable, rhyme relates to identity in the other two positions: peak and coda. Together they can be called the *rhyme* (sometimes spelt *rime*). Two words rhyme if their rhymes (ie peaks and codas) are identical, for instance *plain* and *sane* rhyme, as do *steal* and *kneel*. With words of more than one syllable, everything from the vowel of the stressed syllable onwards must be identical. Thus, *recital* and *title* rhyme (/rɪ'saɪtəl, 'taɪtəl/), as do *eat* and *complete* (/'iːt, kəm'pliːt/). Notice that spelling has nothing to do with this.

Just as there are near-alliterations, so there are near-rhymes, where the rhymes are similar but not quite identical, such as *plain* and *same*. Song lyrics often use near-rhymes, because of the difficulty of finding meaningful perfect rhymes.

Rhymes are an obviously important part of poetry, song lyrics, rapping, and so on. Nursery rhymes are important in that they help children to appreciate the phenomenon of rhyme. The Dr Seuss books, for instance, all depend on rhyme, so much so that even the titles have rhymes – *The Cat in the Hat, Hop on Pop, Fox in Socks, There's a Wocket in my Pocket,* to name a few. The following well-known nursery rhyme shows that spelling is irrelevant: *Simon* and *pieman,* and *fair* and *ware* rhyme, regardless of the difference in spelling.

Simple Simon /ˈsaɪmən/
Met a pieman /ˈpaɪmən/
Going to the fair /ˈfeə/
Said Simple Simon
To the pieman
'Let me taste your ware.' /ˈweə/

Task 6.4 Searching for rhymes (page 77)

You are driving the great /greɪt/ car at the bottom of the page. Make your way to the city /sɪti/ at the top by driving only through the roundabouts containing words that rhyme. You can drive backwards if necessary.

Rhymes and limericks

The limerick is a well-known poetic genre that is often used in English language teaching. Here is an example:

A rocket inventor named Wright
Once travelled much faster than light.
He departed one day
In a relative way
And returned on the previous night.

It has a distinctive form and other characteristics:

- It is humorous, if not bawdy (the above limerick is poking fun at Einstein's theory of relativity).
- It is written as five lines.
- The first, second and last lines rhyme (*Wright, light* and *night*), and the third and fourth lines rhyme (*day* and *way*).
- The first, second and last lines each have three stresses (*rock-, -ven-* and *Wright; trav-, fas-* and *light;* and *–turned, pre-* and *night*), while the third and fourth lines have two each (*-part-* and *day; rel-* and *way*).

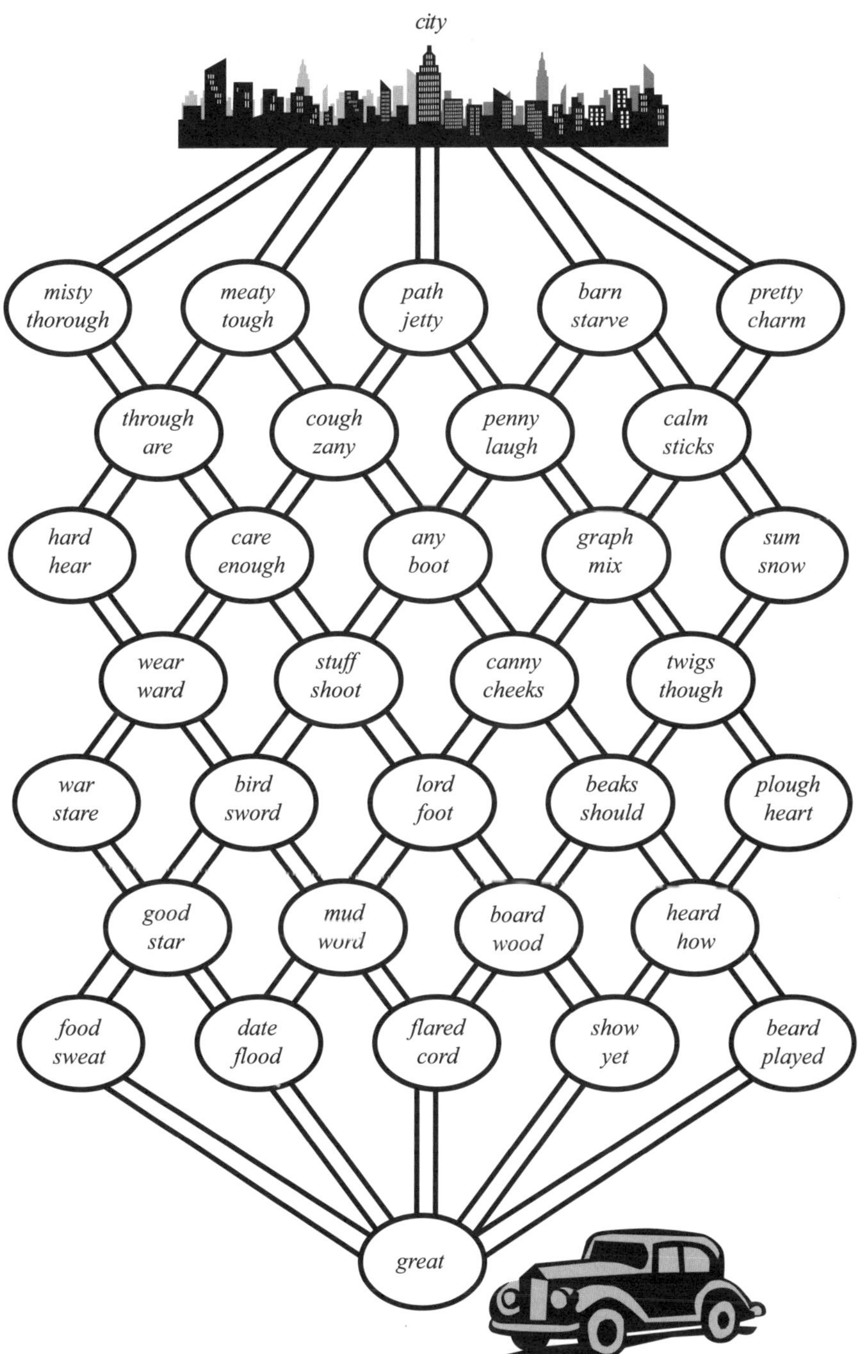
city
misty thorough
meaty tough
path jetty
barn starve
pretty charm
through are
cough zany
penny laugh
calm sticks
hard hear
care enough
any boot
graph mix
sum snow
wear ward
stuff shoot
canny cheeks
twigs though
war stare
bird sword
lord foot
beaks should
plough heart
good star
mud word
board wood
heard how
food sweat
date flood
flared cord
show yet
beard played
great

- The first, second and last lines each have an extra beat (a silent stress) at the end. It is not natural to continue from *Wright* straight into *once*.
- Thus, the limerick is pronounced as follows (with the extra beat shown by Δ):

> A ROCKet inVENtor named WRIGHT Δ
> Once TRAVelled much FASter than LIGHT. Δ
> He dePARTed one DAY
> In a RELative WAY
> And reTURNED on the PREvious NIGHT. Δ

- If we were to rewrite the third and fourth lines together as one line, we would end up with four lines, each with four beats. In other words, this is a very regular poetical form.
- It is also very regular in that the system of beats (feet) is typically a stressed syllable followed by two unstressed syllables, as in *ROCK – et – in, VEN – tor – named*.
- It is also normal to read the limerick with a very regular beat, like a metronome.

Task 6.5 Limericks

For this task, we will concentrate on the fact that the first, second and last lines in a limerick rhyme, as do the third and fourth. Can you provide the missing words at the ends of the following limericks? Since we are talking about sounds, the spelling is irrelevant. If you transcribe the words given (eg *Shepherd* /ʃepəd/), it might therefore help you to find the missing words.

> There was a young hunter named Shepherd
> Who was eaten for lunch by a ________.
> Said the leopard, replete,
> 'He'd have gone down a ________
> If he had been salted and ________!'

> There was a young man from Darjeeling
> Who got on the bus for West Ealing.
> It said on the door
> 'Don't spit on the ________.'
> So he stood up and spat on the ________.

Here are some footballing limericks:

There was a big 'keeper called Walter
Who played on the island of _________.
But his kicks were so long
And the wind was so _________,
That the ball ended up in _________.

There was a young player from Clyde
Took a penalty kick that went _________.
The next week his brother
Squandered _________.
Now neither can get in the _________.

There was a young striker from Reading
Bumped his brow on a door at a _________.
It made his head swell,
But he said 'Just as _________,
'Cos now I'll improve on my _________.'

There was a reserve from Man U
Who seldom had much work to _________.
For a half-hour or so
He'd run to and _________
Then reverse it and run fro and _________.

A striker from A C Milan
Wrote poems that just wouldn't _________.
When told this was so,
He said, 'Yes, I _________,
But I always try to get as many syllables into the last line as I possibly _________.'

Reduplication

There is a process called reduplication that is very productive in certain languages. Sometimes it is used to produce the plural of nouns, as in the following examples:

Malay: *anak* 'child', *anak-anak* 'children'
Thai: /dèk/ 'child', /dèkdèk/ 'children' (this example is given in transcription because Thai uses a different non-Roman alphabet)

In English, the process is not very productive, that is, new examples cannot readily be created. Instead, there are a number of fossilised examples in English vocabulary. They are used for four main purposes:

- to imitate sounds, such as *tick-tock* of a clock
- to suggest alternating movements, such as *ping-pong*
- to disparage by suggesting instability, nonsense, insincerity, vacillation, for example *hob-nob*
- to intensify, as in *teeny-weeny*

Very rarely do English reduplications involve complete repetition of a syllable, for example *ha ha* (laughter), *bye-bye*. Instead, they involve either alternation of the vowel in peak position (eg *tick-tock* /tɪk tɒk/, *ping-pong*) or repetition of the rhyme (peak + coda), that is alternation of the initial consonant(s) in the onset (eg *hob-nob* /hɒb nɒb/, *teeny-weeny*). Occasionally, the latter involves alternation between an empty and a full onset, for instance *airy-fairy* /Øeəri feəri/ (where Ø represents an empty onset). In the two-part expression, both parts may be meaningful (eg *true blue*), or only the first part (eg *super duper*), or sometimes neither part (eg *namby-pamby*). It is irrelevant whether the reduplication is spelt as one word, two words, or hyphenated.

Task 6.6 Reduplication

Can you complete the second part of the following reduplicated expressions? Do they involve alternation of the initial consonant(s) or of the vowel?

*arty-*_____ 'pretentious'	*mish-*_____ 'confused mixture'
*chit-*_____ 'gossip'	*mumbo-*_____ 'nonsense'
*chock-a-*_____ 'very full'	*pitter-*_____ 'noise of rain'
*flip-*_____ 'plastic slippers'	*see*_____ 'playground equipment'
*fuddy-*_____ 'old-fashioned'	*tip-*_____ 'excellent'
*hanky-*_____ 'dishonest behaviour'	*wishy-*_____ 'unclear'

*hip-*_____ 'popular music genre'
*hocus-*_____ 'trickery'
*hoo-*_____ 'fuss'
*hotch*_____ 'untidy mixture'
*hurly-*_____ 'busy situation'
*itsy-*_____ 'very small'
*knick-*_____ 'ornament'

culture _____ 'fan of the arts'
flower _____ 'hippie culture'
from hero to _____ 'fall from grace'
gender _____ 'cross-dresser'
rich _____ 'spoilt female'
ship _____ 'tidy'
bric-a- _____ 'small ornaments'

Task 6.7 Vicars' knickers

For this game, you need to think up two words that rhyme, go together grammatically and make sense, for instance *big pig*. Then you make up clues for the words, in the form of synonyms, near-synonyms or definitions, for example 'large boar'. Your audience has to guess, from your clues, what the rhyming words are.

The words may be sensible pairs that might well be found together (eg *runny honey*) or may be more wacky – this is, after all, a game rather irreverently called *Vicars' Knickers*!

Can you work out, from the following clues, what the rhyming pairs are? In order to emphasise that this game – and indeed the whole concept of rhyming – depends on sounds, not on spellings, I have deliberately chosen rhyming pairs that are spelt differently (like *vicars' knickers*, not like *big pig*).

These first examples involve one-syllable words:

The correct location
A false pain
An army vehicle that doesn't cost much
Half a dozen hits with the foot
A recently created adhesive
A very unattractive fashion
An additional two-plus-two
The trail left by candle drippings
Someone who steals cow meat
A weird person from Athens
Soft leather whose fibres have come apart
A major blood vessel
Which person's holiday by ship?

A pastry dish that's not wet
Things to eat that have been boiled at a low temperature
A solitary painful sound
Part of the arm that has been turned brown by the sun
An indistinct animal with wings
An amphibian that can't speak
Very sensible neckwear

The following examples may involve triphthongs, multi-syllable words, and words with different numbers of syllables (but nonetheless rhyming):

A terrible group of singers
A water-boiler made of copper
An attractive little cat
A sheep that uses its strength to frighten the others
A grass-coloured fish
My brother's daughter, who is very fat
A drunken caravan-dweller
An improved jersey
A boring hypothesis
A language that hasn't existed long
A hip primate
A murderous ape
A fowl with strange habits
Someone who sings sentimental songs on the moon
A water bird's third place prize
A more frightening district
Bubbly wine from Kiev
An African wildlife adventure by moonlight
A senior army officer who comes out at night
A dead vicar

And finally some big big examples:

Something that is very heavy
A very big customer
A very big henchman
A very big dinosaur bone
A very big mushroom

Onsets and slips of the tongue

As we have seen, the syllable can be divided into onset, peak and coda. Furthermore, the link between the peak and coda seems to be stronger than any between the onset and peak. For this reason, the peak and coda are together called the rhyme. The onset gives us instances of alliteration. Both rhyme and alliteration are common devices in languages. For instance, something that is commonplace is called *a dime a dozen* in American English, an instance of alliteration of /d/. In British English, it is *ten a penny*, an instance of the rhyme /en/.

Tongue slips are where what we actually say is not what we intended to say. In other words, it is a performance error: the intended utterance is grammatical, appropriate, and so on, but because our brains are thinking of what to say next while we are speaking, what emerges is usually interfered with by other factors. This may affect whole words, syllables or individual sounds (consonants or vowels).

The commonest type of tongue slip – and probably the most famous type – of tongue slip is the spoonerism, which involves the interference of initial consonants and consonant clusters, that is the onset positions of two words. Spoonerisms are named after Reverend Dr William Archibald Spooner (1844–1930). He attended New College, Oxford, as an undergraduate in 1862, and remained there for over 60 years, as Fellow, lecturer, tutor, Dean and Warden of the college. He was an albino and short-sighted. He was reported as being susceptible to making such slips, not only in speech but also in writing. These characteristics gave him a reputation, and he bore the brunt of the teasing of his students, who invented their own spoonerisms. Many of these have been attributed to Spooner himself, so that it is nowadays difficult to know which ones were actually said by Spooner, and which were inventions of his students and others.

Let us take a spoonerism supposedly said by Spooner in a speech to Queen Victoria, to explain the process:

I have in my bosom a half-warmed fish.

What Spooner meant was *a half-formed wish*. Notice that the /f/ consonant sound at the beginning of *formed* has changed places with the /w/ consonant sound at the beginning of *wish*. Notice also that this is a pronunciation phenomenon, not a spelling one: *formed* contains an *o* letter, while *warmed* contains an *a* letter, but they both represent the /ɔː/ vowel sound.

Spooner was prone to such consonant crossovers (technically known as transpositions), probably because he did not have a good speech monitoring system. We all make tongue slips, but usually correct ourselves immediately, because we monitor what we say as we say it. Most people would not make the spoonerism *a half-warmed fish*, but rather *a half-warmed … er, formed … wish*. In other words, most of us would spot the error (*warmed* for *formed*) and correct it before we reached the second compensatory error (*fish* for *wish*).

To show that this can affect syllable-initial clusters, let us take the following spoonerism, apparently said by Spooner, on proposing a toast:

To our queer old dean!

He meant *to our dear old Queen*. In this example, the single /d/ consonant sound of *dear* has changed with the /kw/ cluster at the beginning of *queen* /kwiːn/.

To show that this can affect whatever is in syllable-initial position, here is another slip attributed to Spooner:

a well-boiled icicle

He was referring to *a well-oiled bicycle*. In this case, the /b/ consonant of *bicycle* has, as it were, changed places with the empty onset position of *oiled*. Thus, using Ø to represent an empty syllable-initial position, we can show this as *a well-Øoiled bicycle* > *a well-boiled Øicicle*.

Occasionally, clusters like this may be broken up, and only part of the cluster changes place. Spooner is reputed to have referred to the British navy as:

cattle ships and bruisers

What he meant was *battleships and cruisers*. Here, there is a /kr/ cluster at the beginning of *cruisers*. However, only the /k/ consonant changes places with the /b/ of *battle*.

It is worth emphasising again that this is a pronunciation phenomenon. Notice the differences in spelling – but not in pronunciation, or therefore transcription – between *formed/warmed*, *dear/queer*, *queen/dean*, and *bicycle/icicle*. In short, these pairs of words rhyme.

Although the term *spoonerism* is usually reserved for the transposition of syllable-initial consonants and consonant clusters, there are many other types of tongue slip. Indeed the only slip that Spooner himself admitted that he remembered having made, in 1879 at age 35, is *Kinkering Congs Their Titles Take* (for *Conquering Kings*, the name of a hymn).

Ironically, this slip involves the transposition of two vowels (/ɒ/ of *conquering* and /ɪ/ of *kings*) and, because it does not involve syllable-initial consonants, would not be called a spoonerism by many writers. Spooner's daughter Rosemary claimed she never heard him utter a spoonerism, and even cast doubt on the *Kinkering Congs* example. Hayter (1977) found 'at least nine fairly authentic first-hand accounts of oral spoonerisms of the traditional kind, involving the transposition of letters [sic] or syllables between words.'

Task 6.8 Spoonerisms

In the following examples (all often attributed to Spooner, but perhaps apocryphal):

- Work out what he meant to say
- Transcribe the intended words
- State which initial consonants or clusters have changed places with which

Slips attributed to Spooner

(To a school official's secretary) Is the bean dizzy?
(Addressing farmers) Ye noble tons of soil.
(During World War I) When the boys come home from France, we'll have hags flung out.
(To a stranger seated in the wrong place) May I sew you to another sheet?
(On visiting a friend's country cottage) You have a nosy little cook here.
The weight of rages will press hard upon the employer.
The Lord is a shoving leopard.
Take this in aid of Oxford's beery wenches.
I saw a student fighting a liar in the quadrangle.
... deal a blushing crow.
... chase the train of thought.
You have hissed all my mystery lectures. You have tasted two worms. Pack up your rags and bugs, and leave immediately by the town drain.

Modern, invented spoonerisms

Go and shake a tower.
You have very mad banners.
It's roaring with pain.
Wave the sails!
I hit my bunny phone.
It crawls through the fax.
..., go help me sod!
monk jail
a damp stealer
a lack of pies
keys and parrots
belly jeans
... and that Charles Dickens' classic *A Sale of Two Titties*!

Task 6.9 What's the difference between ... ?

There is a type of riddle that is based on the same transpositions as tongue slips including spoonerisms. They always begin *What's the difference between ... ?* Let us take some examples and analyse them:

Q: What's the difference between a pianist and a 16-oz weight?
A: A pianist pounds away. The other weighs a pound.
(/paʊndz əweɪ, weɪz ə paʊnd/)

Q: What's the difference between a church bell and a pickpocket?
A: A church bell peals from the steeple. A pickpocket steals from the people.
(/piːlz stiːpəl, stiːlz piːpəl/)

In the first example, the transposition is between /paʊnd/ and /weɪ/, that is syllable-length elements. In the second, the transposition involves initial consonants and consonant clusters (/p/ of *peals* /piːlz/ 'rings' and the /st/ cluster of *steeple* /stiːpəl/), as for spoonerisms proper. Notice that in both cases the transposition involves consonant sounds, regardless of the way they are spelt. Thus, *(a)way* and *weigh* are pronounced the same (/weɪ/) but spelt differently (homophones). And *steeple* and *people* are spelt differently in the middle (*-ee-*, *-eo-*), but their pronunciation is the same (/iː/).

In the following *What's the difference between ... ?* riddles, can you work out the transposition? The first few involve whole syllables or words, while the second section involves spoonerism-like transposition of initial consonants. For the first few, you are given one half of the answer. For the last few, you will have to try to work them out yourself.

Whole syllables/words

Q: What's the difference between a prince and the water in a fountain?
A: A prince is the heir to the throne. Water in a fountain ...

Q: What's the difference between a man who has visited Niagara Falls, and one who has not?
A: A man who has visited Niagara Falls has seen a mist. One who has not ...

Q: What's the difference between a cat and a comma?
A: A cat has claws at the end of its paws. A comma is ...

Q: What's the difference between a married man and a bachelor?
A: A married man kisses his Mrs. A bachelor ...

Initial consonants and clusters

Q: What's the difference between a mouldy lettuce and a dismal song?
A: A mouldy lettuce is a bad salad. A dismal song ...

Q: What's the difference between a cuddle and a louse?
A: A cuddle is a bear hug. A louse ...

Q: What's the difference between a hostile audience and a sick cow?
A: A hostile audience boos madly. A sick cow ...

Q: What's the difference between a squeaking hinge and eggs for breakfast?
A: A squeaking hinge begs to be oiled. The other ...
(*oiled* = *Øoiled*, with an empty onset position)

Q: What's the difference between sticky tape and a stableboy?
A: Sticky tape mends a tear. A stableboy ...

Q: What's the difference between a marksman and a loose-bowelled owl?

Q: What's the difference between a coyote and a flea?

Q: What's the difference between a fisherman and a lazy schoolboy?

Onsets, rhymes and Pig Latin

Pig Latin is a word game played by children. It is especially popular in the USA. It is a way of disguising what you are saying to another Pig Latin-speaking friend in the hope that anyone overhearing you does not understand Pig Latin, or cannot convert it back to regular English quickly enough.

Pig Latin relies on the division of the syllable into its syllable-initial (onset) position and the rhyme, which is composed of the syllable-medial (peak) and syllable-final (coda) positions. The procedure is as follows, taking *cat* as our example word:

- Divide the pronunciation into its onset consonant or consonant cluster, and its rhyme: thus /k/ + /æt/.
- Put the onset after the rhyme: /ætk/.
- Add the /eɪ/ vowel at the end of the word: /ætkeɪ/

If you are perceptive, three queries might have struck you:

- What if there is no consonant or cluster in the onset? The answer is that a dummy consonant is used. Some people use /h/, others use /w/, and others use nothing at all. Thus *ant* /ænt/ would become either /æntheɪ/, /æntweɪ/ or /ænteɪ/, depending on your variety of Pig Latin. It also means that, for some people, *eight* and *hate* both become /eɪtheɪ/, while for others, *eight* and *wait* both become /eɪtweɪ/. We will use /h/ here.
- What if the word has more than one syllable? The answer is that the above conversion is carried out only on the first syllable. Thus *cheetah* /tʃiːtə/ becomes /iːtətʃeɪ/. You do not convert each syllable separately, that is *cheetah* does not become /iːtʃeɪ əteɪ/. So, *Pig Latin* is better known as /ɪgpeɪ ætɪnleɪ/.
- What if the word is a grammatical function word that is usually unstressed and weakened (see Chapter 5)? This often means they are pronounced with the schwa vowel /ə/ rather than a full vowel. In Pig Latin, each word is treated as if it were pronounced in isolation with a full vowel. Thus, *the, and, to, some, must* are pronounced /iːðeɪ, ændheɪ, uːteɪ, ʌmseɪ, ʌstmeɪ/ rather than /əðeɪ, əndheɪ, əteɪ, əmseɪ, əstmeɪ /.

As with so many of the features described in this book, the process is all to do with pronunciation (transcription) and nothing to do with spelling. Thus, *through* and *threw* are both pronounced /uːθreɪ/ in Pig Latin. However, as is often the case, people believe it is to do with, or at least try to represent the pronunciation in, spelling. So, a spelt version of Pig Latin would probably differentiate *ewthray* from *oughthray*.

Task 6.10 Pig Latin

Can you work out the message of these sentences, given in Pig Latin?

1 /uːdeɪ uːjeɪ əʊneɪ ɒtweɪ ɪsðeɪ ezseɪ/

2 /ɔːjeɪ ɒgdeɪ ɪtbeɪ aɪmeɪ egleɪ/

3 /aɪmeɪ aɪfweɪ aɪtsreɪ ɪdzkeɪ ʊksbeɪ/

4 /æŋkθeɪ uːjeɪ eriveɪ ʌtʃmeɪ/

5 /iːzpleɪ ʌdisteɪ ɑːdəheɪ ɔːfeɪ ɔːjeɪ ʌmɪŋkeɪ esttei/

6 /iːðeɪ ɪmɪŋsweɪ uːlpeɪ ɪzheɪ aɪtkweɪ əʊldkeɪ/

7 /uːjeɪ ænkeɪ eɪpleɪ ɔːlheɪ eɪdeɪ ɪðweɪ eɪreɪ/

8 /aɪweɪ ɒtneɪ aɪbeɪ eɪheɪ ɪgəbeɪ ægbeɪ/

Task 6.11 Syllable anagrams

Earlier we had a task entitled *Sound anagrams* (1.11), where the constituent (vowel and consonant) sounds of the words were jumbled. In this task, we are jumbling the syllables of the pronunciation, rather than the individual sounds.

So, can you put these syllables back into the right order to give an English word?

pɑːt	dɪ	mənt
baʊt	ə	raʊnd
pjuː	tə	kəm
fɔːm	əns	pə
grɑːf	fəʊ	tə
wɜːld	əs	feɪm
ʃən	skrɪp	ɪn

nə	əm	tɪz	mæg	
ɪŋ	prə	θɔːt	vəʊk	
vɜːs	nɪ	ti	juː	ə

Syllable structure rules

There are various syllable structure rules (in the sense of generalisations about what does and does not occur) in English, that may help you to transcribe English correctly. Many of these rules are things that you probably already know subconsciously. The purpose of the following task is to try to make some of them conscious.

Task 6.12 Syllable structure rules

1 How many /r/ sounds are there in your pronunciation of the phrase *car park*?
2 Does the word *beige* rhyme with *page* for you?
3 Write down five one-syllable words which have no final consonant sound, eg *bee* /biː/.
4 Write down five words which have a final /ŋ/ sound, eg *bang* /bæŋ/.
5 Write down one word for each of the following initial clusters: /pj-/, /tj-/, /kj-/, /fj-/, /mj-/, /nj-/.

Here are some syllable structure rules for English:

- /ŋ/ is never syllable-initial (in onset) in English. This rule holds for English, but not necessarily other languages. For example, Malay and Thai both allow syllable-initial /ŋ/.
- /h/ is never syllable-final (in coda) in English. Although many words end in an *h* letter in the spelling, this *h* is always either empty (eg *cheetah*) or auxiliary (eg *English, rich*). Other languages, such as Arabic and Malay, allow syllable-final /h/.
- In the phonological analysis adopted here, /w, j/ cannot occur in coda either. They only occur in onset, in words such as *wet* and *yet* /wet, jet/. (Some American analysts propose that words like *go* and *day* have final /w, j/. The arguments for and against this are complicated, and beyond the scope of this book, which concentrates on British analysis of a British accent. However, readers should be aware that they might come across final /w, j/ in American dictionaries.)

- In response to Question 1 in the last task, did you answer none or two? Accents of English worldwide divide into two: those that have two /r/ sounds in *car park*, that allow /r/ in coda (known as *rhotic* accents), and those that have none, that is do not allow it (*non-rhotic*). The British accent we are using as the reference in this book is non-rhotic. As a result, /r/ should not be used in transcriptions unless it is followed by a vowel.
- While the word *car* does not have a final /r/ when said in isolation, it may have one in a phrase such as *car alarm*, where it is followed by a vowel. Such instances are known as linking /r/, and are usually shown in dictionary transcriptions by putting the /r/ in brackets (/kɑː(r)/), or above the line (/kɑːʳ/). The /r/ is not pronounced when the word is said in isolation, or the following word begins with a consonant, as in *car park*.
- Does *beige* rhyme with *page* for you (Question 2)? If so, then you do not have /ʒ/ in coda. Thus, *beige* is /beɪdʒ/. However, *beige*, like many similar words, is a borrowing from French, which has /ʒ/ regularly in coda. Many speakers therefore pronounce it /beɪʒ/. Other words that pattern this way include *barrage, camouflage, collage, cortège, entourage, espionage, fuselage, garage, mirage, montage, rouge*. Similarly, hardly any words of English begin with /ʒ/. The only examples are again French loanwords like *genre, je ne sais quoi* and *joie de vivre* /ʒɒnrə, ʒə nə seɪ kwɑː, ʒwɑː də viːvrə/. So, what can we say about /ʒ/? Perhaps the best we can do is to say that it only occurs in the middle of words (word-medially) such as *vision* /vɪʒən/, but it is a moot point whether this represents a syllable-initial or -final occurrence.
- In a stressed syllable without a final consonant, the vowel must be a long vowel or diphthong (Question 3). English long vowels can occur in closed stressed syllables: *seat, calm, caught, Luke* /siːt, kɑːm, kɔːt, luːk/. They can also occur in open stressed syllables: *see, car, core, lieu* /siː, kɑː, kɔː, luː/. Short vowels, on the other hand, only occur in closed stressed syllables: *sit, come, cot, look* /sɪt, kʌm, kɒt, lʊk/. They do not occur in open stressed syllables. Thus there are no words in English such as /sɪ, kʌ, kɒ, lʊ/.
- If /ŋ/ is a final consonant, then the vowel must be a short vowel: /ɪ/ as in *ring*, /æ/ as in *bang*, /ʌ/ as in *tongue*, or /ɒ/ as in *gong* (Question 4). It cannot be a long vowel. Thus /ɑːŋ, ɜːŋ, uːŋ, eəŋ, aʊŋ/ and so on all sound un-English.
- If, in a two-consonant initial cluster, the second consonant is /j/ (Question 5), then the vowel is /uː, ʊə/ in stressed syllables, for

example *pure, tune, cute, few, mural, new* /pjʊə, tjuːn, kjuːt, fjuː, mjʊərəl, njuː/ (or /ʊ, ə/ in unstressed, eg *regular* /regjʊlə/). There are very few exceptions to this rule, for instance possible pronunciations of *piano, fjord*.

- In two-consonant (nasal + consonant) final clusters that do not involve an *-s* or *-ed* suffix, there is agreement between the nasal and the following consonant in terms of place of articulation. If the nasal is /m/, then the following consonant is bilabial or labio-dental, for example *jump, triumph* /dʒʌmp, traɪʌmf/. If the nasal is /n/, then the following consonant is alveolar or palato-alveolar, for example *land, inch* /lænd, ɪntʃ/. If the nasal is /ŋ/, then the following consonant is velar, for example *think* /θɪŋk/. Don't be fooled into thinking that the *n* letter in *think* is really an alveolar /n/ sound.
- The *-s* suffix is pronounced as:
  - /ɪz/ when it follows /s, z, ʃ, ʒ, tʃ, dʒ/, as in *passes, buzzes, wishes, garages, watches, hedges*. This adds an extra syllable to the stem.
  - /s/ when it follows voiceless consonants (other than /s, ʃ, tʃ/), as in *raps, hits, laughs*
  - /z/ when it follows voiced consonants (other than /z, ʒ, dʒ/) and vowels, as in *rubs, loves, runs, goes*
- The *-ed* suffix is pronounced as:
  - /ɪd/ when it follows /t, d/, as in *wanted, handed*. This adds an extra syllable to the stem.
  - /t/ when it follows voiceless consonants (other than /t/), as in *liked, sketched, rushed*
  - /d/ when it follows voiced consonants (other than /d/) and vowels, as in *robbed, lived, jammed, feared*

7

Practice tasks

This chapter contains a number of tasks which may be used in different ways. Readers who need more practice at phonemic symbols can simply try them out themselves. Readers who are English teachers can use them in class, as a means of familiarising students with symbols. The tasks must, of course, be adapted according to the students' age and level.

Task 7.1 Phonemic Bingo

Bingo is usually played with numbers. Players have cards with numbers on them. Someone calls out numbers at random, and the players cross off the numbers on their cards if they are the same. The first player to cross off a row of numbers wins.

We can adapt this by using phonemic symbols rather than numbers. Give the students the following card, and tell them to blank out any six squares, leaving four squares per row.

ɒ	iː	ɑː	dʒ	m	ɔɪ
n	k	s	e	aɪ	l
ʃ	eə	ʌ	tʃ	ʊ	r

The cards may therefore look like this:

Player 1

ɒ	■	ɑː	■	m	ɔɪ
■	k	s	e	■	l
ʃ	eə	■	tʃ	ʊ	■

Player 2

	iː		dʒ	m	ɔɪ
n		s	e	aɪ	
ʃ	eə	ʌ			r

The teacher then reads out a list of words. The students listen carefully, and cross out any sounds that they hear. The sounds may be vowels and/or consonants. So, the word *team* /tiːm/ would allow the second player to cross out both the /iː/ and the /m/. The first player to cross out a whole row wins.

Task 7.2 Phonemic Snap

We all know the children's game Snap. Players take turns to put down cards one on top of the other. When cards with the same picture are put down, the first player to shout 'Snap!' takes the cards. The first player to collect all the cards wins.

We can adapt Snap to practise thinking of sounds. The cards still contain pictures, but instead of thinking about matching the pictures, we think about whether the words for the pictures contain the same vowel sounds. A pack of cards needs to be prepared, therefore, containing pictures such as the following:

Vowel sound	Pictures
/iː/	*cheese, feet, tree, key, teeth, police*
/ɪ/	*hill, milk, film, fist, ship, six*
/e/	*bed, ten, desk, net, pen, bell*
/æ/	*hand, hat, bag, badge, cab, axe*
/ɑː/	*car, bath, branch, heart, half, farm*
etc	

Task 7.3 Phonemic Boggle

You probably know the game Boggle. It is quite popular in English language teaching. It involves 16 dice showing letters of the alphabet on all their faces. The dice are then shaken up, giving 16 randomly-chosen letters to work with. Participants have to make as many words as they can using those 16 letters in a time limit. Whoever creates the most words wins.

We can create a game along the same lines, but using phonemic symbols rather than letters of the alphabet. Participants use the symbols (sounds) to create as many words of English as they can.

Phonemic Boggle game 1

How many words of English can you make using the sounds /æ, k, s, t/? Symbols can be used more than once, for instance *stats* (a common abbreviation of *statistics*) uses the /s/ and /t/ sounds twice. I found 28 different sound sequences, representing 43 different spellings, because of homophones, often involving placement of an apostrophe. So you should be able to find at least a dozen. Here are a couple to start you off:

sacked /sækt/
taxed /tækst/

Phonemic Boggle game 2

Let us repeat the first game, but this time using the vowel sound /ɒ/ instead of /æ/. How many words can you think of now? Here are a couple to start you off:

costs /kɒsts/
tossed /tɒst/

Task 7.4 Phonemic word chains

A game commonly found in newspapers, puzzle books, and so on, it involves going from one word eventually to another word, in a small number of steps, each time by changing one letter in the spelling. For instance, you can change *lose* into *find* in four steps, as follows:

LOSE
LONE
LINE
FINE
FIND

Of course, this puzzle works with spelling – you are changing one letter in the spelling at each step. The puzzle below works with pronunciation – you change one sound in the pronunciation (one phonemic symbol in the transcription) at each step. For example, we can change *teach* /tiːtʃ/ into *learn* /lɜːn/ in three steps:

/tiːtʃ/	*teach*
/liːtʃ/	*leech*
/lɜːtʃ/	*lurch*
/lɜːn/	*learn*

Notice that one sound (phonemic symbol) changes at each step (/t/ > /l/, /iː/ > /ɜː/, /tʃ/ > /n/). The spelling is irrelevant in this puzzle, for instance the vowels in *teach* and *leech*, and *lurch* and *learn* are spelt differently.

Change the following initial words into the final words in the number of steps indicated. Definitions of the missing intervening words are given to help you.

Change *kiss* into *cheek*
in three steps

/kɪs/	*kiss*
/ /	'hit with the foot'
/ /	'baby chicken'
/tʃiːk/	*cheek*

Change *room* into *wall*
in three steps

/ruːm/	*room*
/ /	'where a baby grows'
/ /	'less than hot'
/wɔːl/	*wall*

Change *rinse* into *washed*
in six steps

/rɪns/	*rinse*
/ /	'meat in very small pieces'
/ /	'plant for flavouring'
/ /	'supposed (to)'
/ /	'travelled'
/ /	'desire'
/wɒʃt/	*washed*

Change *stage* into *fright*
in six steps

/steɪdʒ/	*stage*
/ /	'declare'
/ /	'stone roof tile'
/ /	'flat round dish'
/ /	'sad/difficult situation'
/ /	'journey through air'
/fraɪt/	*fright*

Change *waist* into *band* in seven steps		Change *class* into *school* in seven steps	
/weɪst/	*waist*	/klɑːs/	*class*
/ /	'glue'	/ /	'office worker'
/ /	'create a picture'	/ /	'short high sound'
/ /	'Christian holy person'	/ /	'fastener'
/ /	'perfume'	/ /	'careless mistake'
/ /	'curved or twisted'	/ /	'jump over a rope'
/ /	'make something curved'	/ /	'ability'
/bænd/	*band*	/skuːl/	*school*

? Task 7.5 Phonemic Scrabble

We are all familiar with the board game Scrabble. It was originally developed by an American, Alfred Mosher Butts, in 1931. After refinements (and several changes of name, from Lexico to New Anagrams, Alph, Criss-Cross then Criss-Crosswords), all the main features of the modern game (the 15 x 15 board, the seven-tile rack, the distribution and the values of the letters) have remained the same since 1938.

To play Phonemic Scrabble:

1 Use a regular Scrabble board and tiles.

2 Stick the following phonemic symbols and scores on the tiles:

Symbol and score	ə 1	ɪ 1	e 1	aɪ 1	ʌ 1	eɪ 1
No. of tiles	10	8	3	2	2	2

Symbol and score	iː 2	əʊ 2	æ 2	ɒ 2	ɔː 2	uː 2
No. of tiles	1	1	1	1	1	1

Symbol and score	ʊ 2	ɑː 2	aʊ 2	ɜː 2	n 1	t 1
No. of tiles	1	1	1	1	8	7

Symbol and score	d 1	s 1	l 1	ð 1	r 1	m 2
No. of tiles	5	5	4	3	4	3

Symbol and score	k 2	w 2	z 3	v 3	b 3	f 3
No. of tiles	3	3	2	2	2	2

Symbol and score	p 3	h 4	ŋ 4	g 4	ʃ 4	* 0
No. of tiles	2	1	1	1	1	4

* A blank tile, which can be used for any sound, but does not score.

3 Follow the usual Scrabble rules, including double- and treble-scoring squares.

Notes

- Not all of the vowel and consonant sounds have been used. The rarest ones have been omitted.
- The highest-scoring tile in Phonemic Scrabble is four points, whereas in Scrabble proper Q and Z are worth ten points, and J and X eight. Since there are no very high-scoring tiles, overall scores will be somewhat less than in Scrabble proper.
- Use a reputable dictionary as the reference dictionary for confirmation of disputable answers.
- Notice how the values and number of tiles relate to the tables of text frequencies given on pages 52 and 53.

Task 7.6 Phonemic wordsearch

The puzzle on page 99 contains 22 English first names, written in transcription. They may be horizontal, vertical or diagonal in any direction. For instance, the girl's name *Janice* is highlighted in the first row. Clues beneath the puzzle will help you know what you are searching for.

dʒ	æ	n	ɪ	s	uː	r	b
ɒ	e	ə	k	ɪ	n	ɒ	m
n	ə	f	ɪ	n	e	dʒ	ə
d	eɪ	v	ɪ	d	l	dʒ	d
æ	ɪ	k	ɒ	i	s	uː	ɒ
n	əʊ	r	ɪ	tʃ	ə	d	n
l	ə	k	aɪ	m	n	i	ə

______ Aykroyd, Canadian actor
______ Blume, children's book writer
______ Bridges, film star of *Seabiscuit* and *The Fabulous Baker Boys*
______ Copperfield, the magician
______ Crawford, model and actress
______ Diesel, star of *XXX*
______ Jackson, pop singer of *Thriller* and *Bad*
______ Jagger of the Rolling Stones
______ Johnson, of the 1980s TV series *Miami Vice*
______ Kidman, Australian actress
______ Law, film star of *Gattaca, Artificial Intelligence: AI* and *Sky Captain and the World of Tomorrow*
______ Lennon, of the Beatles
______ Lopez, actress, singer and dancer
______ Mandela, former president of South Africa
______ Nixon, former US president
______ Nolte, film star of *48 Hours* and *Down and Out in Beverly Hills*
______ Seles, tennis player
______ Stewart, pop singer
______ Townsend, author of the Adrian Mole books
______, the Material Girl singer turned children's book writer
______ Willis, of the *Die Hard* films

Task 7.7 Phonemic crosswords

We are all familiar with the crossword format. The crosswords below are exactly the same, except that the answers have to be entered in transcription, not in spelling. They go from simple to tough.

Crossword 1

1		2
	■	
3		

Across

1 Leave something in liquid

3 Unable to walk properly

Down

1 Earth

2 Not showing worry

Crossword 2

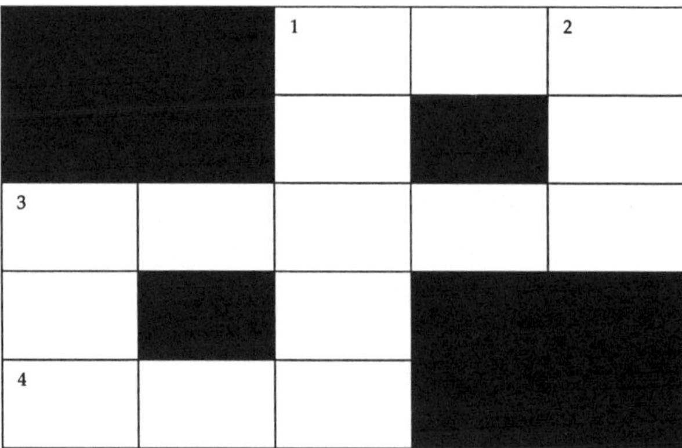

Across

1 Poem

3 Furniture for storage

4 For example, 8 June

Down

1 Furry animal with long ears

2 How you are feeling

3 Was able to

Crossword 3

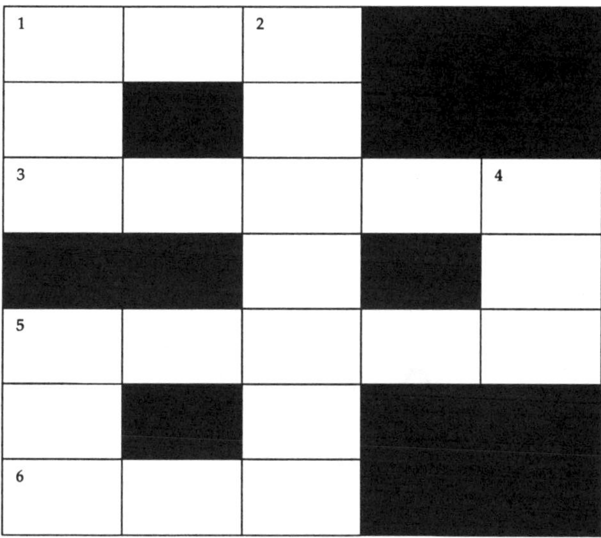

Across

1 Plant used in cooking
3 _____ Branagh, British actor
5 Win a victory over someone
6 Where you play tennis

Down

1 A long walk in the country
2 Advantage
4 Idea
5 Floor of a ship

Crossword 4

1		2		3	■	■	4		5		6
	■		■	7				■		■	
8					■	■	9				
	■		■	10				■		■	
11	12		13		■	■	14	15		16	
■		■		■	■	■	■		■		■
■		■		■	■	■	■		■		■
17		18		19	■	■	20		21		22
	■		■	23				■		■	
24					■	■	25				
	■		■	26				■		■	
27					■	■	28				

Across

1 Someone who flies an aircraft
4 A small piece of paper
7 Money or property owned by a company
8 Hitting a golfball when near the hole
9 In a straight standing position
10 The actors in a film or play
11 Remove parts of a book or film for moral or political reasons
14 Burning with a lot of flames
17 The official who fires a gun to begin a race
20 A baby _____ tightly to its mother when it is afraid
23 A long narrow strip of cloth with folds, used as decoration
24 Small
25 A word like *quickly* that modifies a verb or adjective
26 Possessing
27 The part of a book that consists of writing, not pictures
28 A small flat object that you put under a cup to protect the table

Down

1 Aim, intention, objective
2 Language of the ancient Romans
3 A large ship or truck that carries petrol or oil
4 If you t-t-talk like this when n-n-nervous, you ____
5 Relating to the countryside
6 People in stations or hotels who carry your bags
12 Make a book ready for publication by correcting the mistakes
13 One hundredth of a dollar
15 A reading system for blind people that uses small raised marks that they feel with their fingers
16 If your body is giving you a continuous pain, it is _____
17 Divide something into several parts
18 The northernmost part of the world
19 Resting on water, not submerged
20 The short loud sound of a heavy metal object
21 A document giving details of goods or services that someone has bought and must pay for
22 You should cross the road at a _____ crossing

Task 7.8 Phonemic Hangman

We are all familiar with the game Hangman. The rules are quite simple:

1 The first person thinks of a word, and puts a number of blanks on paper, corresponding to the number of letters in the spelling of the word. So, if the mystery word is *station*, seven blanks are given:

___ ___ ___ ___ ___ ___ ___

2 The second person then guesses a letter of the alphabet that they think is contained in the spelling of the word.

3 If that letter is indeed in the spelling, the first person enters it (more than once, if there is more than one example of the letter in the spelling, eg the two *ts* in *station*) in the appropriate place(s) in the blanks.

4 If the letter is not contained in the spelling of the word, the first person writes the letter somewhere else (so that the second person does not guess that wrong letter again), and draws the first stroke of the following picture.

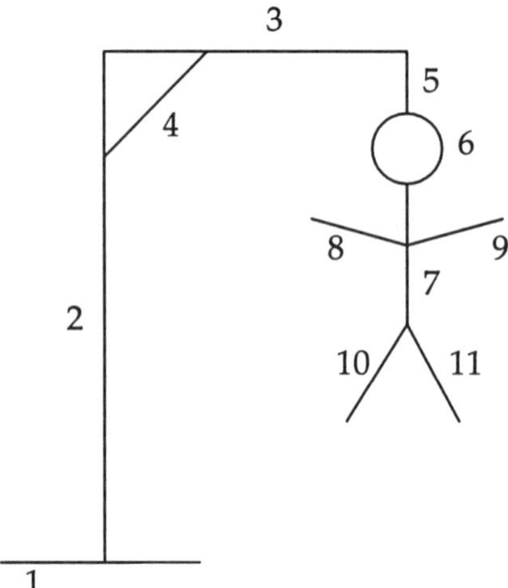

5 The game continues until either the second person guesses the word correctly, and wins, or the hangman picture is complete, that is the second person has made 11 wrong guesses, and loses.

This is essentially the same game format as television's *Wheel of Fortune,* except that in *Wheel of Fortune* a hangman picture is not drawn and there is no limit to the number of wrong guesses.

In order to concentrate on sounds rather than spelling, we can play exactly the same game, except that the blanks for the mystery word represent the sounds in its pronunciation. So, if the mystery word is *station,* only six blanks are given, representing the sounds /s t eɪ ʃ ə n/:

__ __ __ __ __ __

To make it easier to refer to individual sounds when guessing, a chart such as that given on page vii can be used.

In *Wheel of Fortune,* the most useful letters to guess (ie the ones that are most likely to occur in the spelling of words of English) are the vowel letter E, and the consonant letters R, S, T, L and N. These are the ones that are given for free in the final jackpot round. It will soon become obvious that the best vowels to begin guessing with in Phonemic Hangman are those at the top of the frequency charts given on pages 52 and 53, namely /ə, ɪ/. And the best consonants are /n, t, d, s/.

8

Tips for correct transcription

The aim of this book is to help readers become familiar with phonemic symbols, so that they can read transcriptions in dictionaries, and be able to work out what pronunciation the transcriptions represent. In other words, the focus is on perception.

Nevertheless, we imagine that readers may, on occasion, be required to write pronunciations in transcription, that is production. What follows is a number of tips to help readers avoid the pitfalls of phonemic transcription of English sounds. Most of these tips have been mentioned before in the book, or follow on from previous discussion. They are therefore a handy checklist for when readers have occasion to produce transcriptions.

General pointers

Bear in mind that there are hardly any exceptionless spelling-to-sound rules for English (or sound-to-spelling). The following tips account for large numbers of words, but may have counter-examples.

1 Never use /c, q, x, y/ as phonemic symbols.

2 'Silent' letters do not represent a sound in the pronunciation and therefore should not be represented by a phonemic symbol in the transcription.

3 The names of letters of the alphabet, as in initialisms, need to be transcribed, as do numbers, for example MP3 /em piː θriː/.

4 Do not capitalise phonemic symbols, for instance *March* the month and *march* the verb are both pronounced the same, and therefore both /mɑːtʃ/.

5 Homophones, because they are pronounced the same, have the same transcription.

6 Homographs, because they are pronounced in two different ways, have two different transcriptions.

7 French has almost as bad an alphabetic spelling system as English, in terms of poor sound-to-letter correspondence, and the existence of 'silent' letters. Be careful, therefore, with loanwords from French and other languages.

8 The way you transcribe a loanword should be the regular English way of pronouncing it, not the way it is pronounced in the original language (if you happen to know this).

9 Do not try to remember the sounds of phonemic symbols by using spelling clues, such as the /ɪə/ vowel is 'ear'. The spelling *ear* can represent several different vowel phonemes. If this strategy worked, dictionaries would use it.

Consonants

1 For the indefinite article, *a* (/ə/ unstressed, /eɪ/ stressed) occurs before consonant sounds, *an* (/ən/ unstressed, /æn/ stressed) before vowel sounds.

2 The letter *x* represents /ks, gz/. Where a consonant sound follows in the pronunciation, it is usually /ks/, as in *extra, excite* /ekstrə, ɪksaɪt/. Where a vowel sound follows, the pronunciation depends on stress placement. If the stress falls on the preceding vowel, it usually represents /ks/, as in *flexible, maximum* /'fleksəbəl, 'mæksɪməm/. If the stress falls on the following vowel, *x* usually represents /gz/, as in *exist, exam* /ɪg'zɪst, ɪg'zæm/. At the end of a word, it is always /ks/, as in *tax, fox* /tæks, fɒks/.

3 The letter sequence *qu* usually represents /kw/, as in *quick* /kwɪk/. In French loanwords, it may represent /k/, as in *quiche* /ki:ʃ/.

4 In words ending *-mb* in the spelling, the *b* is always 'silent', for example *limb* /lɪm/.

5 In words beginning *kn-* in the spelling, the *k* letter is always 'silent', for example *knife* /naɪf/.

6 A *g* letter is not always a /g/ sound. It may also be /dʒ/ (eg *ginger*), part of /ŋ/ (*sing*) or 'silent' (*sign*). In words that start *gn-* (*gnaw*), it is always 'silent'.

7 The dental fricatives /θ, ð/ are always spelt *th*, for example *think, this* /θɪŋk, ðɪs/.

8 The *th* letter sequence only represents /t/ in *Anthony, Esther, Lesotho, Thailand, Thames, Theresa, Thomas, thyme.*

9 The letter *s* is the commonest spelling for both /s, z/. Be careful, especially in syllable-final position. The following rules may help:
- If it is spelt with a *z* or *zz*, it is a /z/, as in *prize, jazz.*
- If it is spelt with a *ce,* it is an /s/, as in *price.*
- If it is spelt with *ss,* it is /s/, as in *pass.*
- If it is a plural noun, third person singular present tense verb, possessive, or abbreviation of *is* or *has,* use the rule in 10 below.
- Otherwise, there is no rule, so use a dictionary to check.

10 The *-s* suffix for regular nouns and verbs is /ɪz/ after /s, z, ʃ, ʒ, tʃ, dʒ/ (eg *passes*), /s/ after other voiceless consonants (*raps*) and /z/ after other voiced consonants and vowels (*rubs, laws*).

11 The *-ed* suffix for regular verbs is /ɪd/ after /t, d/ (eg *wanted*), /t/ after other voiceless consonants (*liked*) and /d/ after other voiced consonants and vowels (*robbed, cheered*).

12 Do not start or end a word with /ʒ/. The only exceptions are a few French loanwords (eg *genre, camouflage*), provided you pronounce them with /ʒ/ rather than /dʒ/. In short, /ʒ/ normally occurs in the middle of words (*vision*).

13 Do not end a word with /h/. It is never syllable-final in English. Word-final *h* letters are always 'silent' (eg *cheetah*) or part of *sh* (*English*), *ch* (*such*), *th* (*myth*), *ph* (*graph*) or *gh* (*laugh*).

14 Do not start a word with /ŋ/. It is never syllable-initial in English.

15 Do not write /ŋ/ unless it is preceded by a short vowel.

16 An *n* letter before a velar /k, g/ is normally /ŋ/ rather than /n/.

17 Remember that the /j/ phonemic symbol does not represent the sound in *jaw* /dʒɔː/. It represents the sound in *your* /jɔː/.

18 Do not end a word with /w, j/. They are never syllable-final in the analysis of English sounds underlying transcriptions in British dictionaries.

19 Do not write /r/ unless it is followed by a vowel sound. This may be in syllable-initial position (eg *red, disrupt*) or as linking /r/ (*clear up*). Elsewhere, there is no /r/ in non-rhotic accents, for example *car* /kɑː/.

Vowels

1 Do not end a word with a short vowel (/ɪ, e, æ, ʌ, ɔ, ʊ/). *Hair* must therefore be /heə/ rather than /he/.

2 The letter *i* by itself rarely represents /iː/. It is usually /ɪ/, for example *bit*.

3 In stressed syllables, the letter *e* only represents /ɪ/ in the exceptional words *English, pretty*. It is usually /e/, for example *ten*.

4 The /eɪ/ vowel is seldom spelt with an *e* letter, or combinations involving *e*. The main exceptions are French loanwords, such as *suede, foyer, ballet, puree, cliché*. The spelling *ea* only occurs in three words: *break, great, steak* (all of which have more regularly spelt homophones in *brake, grate, stake*).

5 The /æ/ vowel is always spelt with an *a* letter. The only two words where the *a* letter represents /e/ are *any* and *many*.

6 The *ar* letter sequence cannot represent /æ/.

7 The /ʌ/ vowel is never spelt with an *a* letter.

8 The *a* letter, following a /w/ sound, is often /ɒ/, as in *want, squash* /wɒnt, skwɒʃ/. It may also be /æ/, as in *wax* /wæks/.

9 The *ar* letter combination following a /w/ sound is often pronounced as /ɔː/, for example *quarter* /kwɔːtə/.

10 The *o* letter by itself (not in combinations such as *or, ough*) never represents /ɔː/.

11 The /ɒ/ vowel is never represented by a letter combination involving *r*.

12 An *o* letter before an *l* letter is more usually /əʊ/ (eg *dole* /dəʊl/) rather than /ɒ/ (eg *doll* /dɒl/). The /əʊ/ vowel, when preceding a 'dark' /l/, changes to resemble the /ɒ/ vowel for many speakers. Thus, it may not be obvious that the word *Pole* contains /əʊ/ rather than /ɒ/. However, it becomes obvious from the word *Poland*, where the /əʊ/ now ends the first syllable (/pəʊ.lənd/) and is not affected by the darkness of the following /l/ (because, now being syllable-initial, it is clear).

13 The /ʊ, uː/ vowels are not well distinguished in spelling, for instance they can both be *oo* (*good, food* /gʊd, fuːd/).

14 The *ow* letter sequence may represent both /əʊ, aʊ/, as in *grown, growl* /grəʊn, graʊl/.

15 The centring diphthongs /ɪə, eə, ʊə/ are usually followed by an /r/ consonant (eg *hero*) or contain a following *r* letter, as in *care*, which

would therefore always be pronounced by rhotic speakers. *Hero* is thus /hɪərəʊ/ rather than /hiːrəʊ/.

16 The /ʊə/ vowel is not only the least common in connected speech. It is also being replaced in many words by /ɔː/ by many speakers, as in *sure* /ʃʊə, ʃɔː/. It is thus likely to disappear from the vowel inventory eventually.

17 The triphthongs /eɪə, aɪə, ɔɪə, əʊə, aʊə/ are not common and have arguable status. Some have become diphthongs in some words, as a result of 'smoothing', for example *mayor* /meɪə, meə/. Compare *layer* /leɪə/ with *prayer* /preə/.

18 The symbols /i, u/ can be used for unstressed vowels in the high front and high back regions, as in *happy, punctuation* /hæpi, pʌŋktʃueɪʃən/.

Stress

1 Do not use /ə/ in a stressed syllable. What you mean is probably /ɜː/, for example *certain* /ˈsɜːtən/.

2 The schwa vowel /ə/ has no regular spelling correspondence, and can be represented by a variety of spellings.

3 Many grammatical function words, such as *the, a, to, from, at, as, must, and, but,* usually contain the schwa vowel /ə/ because they are usually unstressed in connected speech (thus /ðə, ə, tə, frəm, ət, əz, məst, ənd, bət/).

4 Words with the endings spelt *-ity, -ic,* or pronounced /-ʃən/ usually have the stress on the syllable preceding these endings.

5 The placement of stress is part of the overall phonological shape of multi-syllable words. The stress placement must therefore be learnt, along with the consonants and vowels, when learning the pronunciation of unfamiliar words.

If all else fails, remember that the word you want to transcribe is in the dictionary, unless it is a rare or technical word, or a small dictionary. And all entries in English dictionaries for learners give you a transcription.

9

Literacy and spelling reform

On the assumption that many of the readers of this book are either learners of English or teachers of English, this chapter gives some comments about literacy, that is the ability to read and write. Spelling reform is also touched on, since this would improve literacy and largely obviate the need for phonemic symbols.

Literacy

Many topics are nowadays subsumed under the heading of literacy, such as critical literacy, IT literacy, visual literacy, multi-literacies and the differences in language used by and to males and females. However, in this section, we are dealing with the core concept of literacy, as the ability to read and write. Or, to look at it from the opposite perspective, avoiding illiteracy. This is a process that we have all been through (since you are reading this book written by me), and one that is considered crucial at an early age (kindergarten or lower primary level) because illiteracy is a severe handicap in life.

Literacy depends on many factors, not all of them to do with linguistic features of the language. The importance given to literacy in a society, the funding made available by governments for literacy teaching, the way literacy teaching is handled by the educational system of a country, the quality of books and other materials used in schools, or simply the knowledge, motivation and teaching provided by a particular teacher, may all have an effect on the success of a particular learner or of a whole society.

However, one cannot ignore linguistic factors contributing to success in literacy in a particular language. Chinese is considered a difficult language to learn to read and write, because, having a logographic writing system, it involves a huge number of characters which have to be learnt by heart. In contrast, languages that use the roman alphabet require the learning of only 26 letter shapes (or 52, if we consider capitals and lower-case letters separately). While English uses an alphabetic system, the correspondences between sounds and letters are poor, with many exceptions (see the list for the letter *c* in Chapter 2). As a result, the spelling system is difficult, and a lot of classroom time has to be devoted to spelling. Even educated adult speakers (including famous writers) continue to make spelling mistakes, and it is the subject of jokes.

> You write a swell letter. Glad somebody spells worse than I do.
>
> (Ernest Hemingway, in a letter to F Scott Fitzgerald, both poor spellers)

> The three [letters] you wrote me after I had broken off the engagement are so beautiful, and so badly spelled, that even now I can hardly read them without crying a little.
>
> (Cecily, in Oscar Wilde's *The Importance of Being Earnest*)

> ... my spelling is Wobbly. It's good spelling but it Wobbles, and the letters get in the wrong places.
>
> (Winnie-the-Pooh, in A A Milne's *Winnie-the-Pooh*)

In contrast, the spelling systems of languages with good sound-to-spelling correspondences, such as Spanish, Finnish and Malay, are simple to learn and use. As a result of this, there are many advantages that languages with simple spelling systems have over English (the following examples all relate to Malay):

- It is difficult to give accurate literacy figures for countries that use Malay and those that use English, because there are many other factors involved aside of linguistic ones (see above), and many countries do not divulge official statistics. However, it is generally acknowledged that children who are native speakers of Malay master its spelling system after six months to one year of schooling. In comparison, children who are native speakers of English take many years and often never fully master it.
- It may come as a surprise to readers that Malay dictionaries do not typically include phonemic transcriptions showing how words are pronounced. The Malay spelling system is, in effect, a phonemic transcription. In contrast, these transcriptions are a necessary feature of all English dictionaries. Indeed, many learners of English resent the fact that they are required to become familiar with phonemic transcription symbols (in addition to learning the spelling of words) in order to use a dictionary effectively for this purpose.

- There is no problem in looking up a word in a Malay dictionary. If a word begins with, say, a /w/ sound, it must be located in the W section of the dictionary. In contrast, learners of English are often confronted with the dilemma 'How can I look up the word if I don't know how to spell it?' For instance, who in their right mind would think of looking for the words /nəʊm, ɒnɪst, naɪf, wʌns, fəʊn/ in the G, H, K, O and P sections, rather than N, O, N, W and F?
- It follows from the many-to-one and one-to-many correspondence between sounds and letters in English that there exist homophones and homographs (see Chapter 4). In contrast, since the Malay system is almost perfectly one-to-one, there are no homophones, and very few homographs (eg *perang* = /pəraŋ/ 'war' or /peraŋ/ 'brown (hair)'). There may, however, be homonyms in both languages.
- Similarly, there are no sight-rhymes in Malay, that is words which from their spelling look as though they should rhyme but do not in fact. Such sight-rhymes are common in (albeit older, more traditional) English rhymes.

  There were two crows sat on a stone. /stəʊn/
  One flew away and then there was one. /wʌn/
  The one, seeing his neighbour gone, /gɒn/
  He flew away, and then there were none. /nʌn/

- In Malay, there is no scope for spelling pronunciations. These are examples in English where speakers pronounce a word the way it is spelt, only to find that the word is irregularly spelt, because of 'silent' letters, and so on. For instance, many foreign learners pronounce *salmon* with an /l/ sound, misled understandably by the fact that there is an *l* letter in the spelling.
- Spelling bees are especially popular in the USA. Students are required to recite the correct spelling of words of increasing difficulty, not only in terms of their rarity as words, but also in terms of the irregularity of their spelling. Spelling bee champions exhibit great powers of memorisation. In Malay, the concept of a spelling bee does not exist. If a word is pronounced a certain way, then it must be spelt a certain way. There is no uncertainty, and no need to memorise lists of difficult words – all words are equally simple in terms of their spelling.

A major problem with spelling in English language classrooms is that teachers often tackle the problem by simply giving out lists of words whose spelling is to be learnt. However, teachers seldom give any guidance as to ***how*** learners should learn the spelling. There are various strategies based on different types of awareness that can be (or must be) used for coping with English spelling:

- ***Phonological*** (phonemic, phonetic) awareness underlies the basic alphabetic principle of English spelling and the phonics approach, namely that letters represent sounds. It has many components. It involves not only the ability to segment words into their constituent syllables (thus /dɪpɑːtmənt/ > /dɪ – pɑːt – mənt/), but also to segment the syllables into their onset and rhyme (thus /pɑːt/ > /p – ɑːt/), and the onset and rhyme into their constituent individual sounds (/p – ɑː – t/). This is a prerequisite to being able to associate these individual sounds with their (probable) spellings, for example the /p/ and /t/ sounds are regularly spelt with *p* and *t* letters, and /ɑː/ is often *ar* (60% of the time according to Carney, 1994).

  The spelling of *part* may be related to the spelling of other words with the same rhyme (peak + coda), such as *chart, smart, start, tart*.

  Some writers extend phonological awareness to include awareness of related forms. For instance, the fact that the vowel letter in the final syllable of *department* is spelt with *e* (and not, say *a* as in *adamant)* is obvious when you consider the related word *departmental,* which has a full /e/ vowel sound.

  Carney (1994:102) points out that an awareness of other accents of English may help: 'Anyone who knows that an American would say *tomato* with their equivalent of /eɪ/ would not be tempted to spell *tomato* as **tomarto*.'

- ***Visual*** imagery involves rote learning of the visual shape of the word, with little attention to the letter-to-sound correspondence. This underlies the 'look – cover – write – check' strategy, and can be called spelling by eye rather than spelling by ear or mouth. That is, English writers commonly write out various possible spellings of a difficult word and then look at them to see which one looks right.

  While both phonological and visual processes are needed in English, 'good spellers at all ages display a better understanding of phonological rules and orthographic patterns than poor spellers, and more frequently use a phonological as opposed to a visual approach to spelling' (Lennox & Siegel, 1994:99).

  A visual approach is necessary for English words like *one, choir,* that are simply too irregular for any other approach.

- ***Morphemic*** awareness involves considering the fact that English regularly makes words by adding affixes to other words, for example *photograph, photography, photographic.* English tends to keep the same spelling for the stem regardless of any added affixes, and regardless of any changes in pronunciation, for example the stress, vowel and consonant changes in /ˈfəʊtəgrɑːf, fəˈtɒgrəfi, fəʊtəˈgræfɪk/. In many respects, this reflects the historical development of words, and led Chomsky and Halle (1968:49) to describe English spelling as 'near optimal'.
- Spelling by ***analogy*** involves writers using their knowledge of other words of English to predict the probable spelling of new words. In the case of research into spelling, these are often non-existent words. 'For example, when [children were] asked to spell *sike* they remarked that it resembled the word *like* and that *hamily* was just like *family*' (Goulandris, 1994:417).
- ***Etymological*** awareness involves writers knowing the historical origins of words. Since this type of knowledge is not common knowledge for English speakers, errors because of etymological ignorance (part of what is known as folk etymology) can occur.

> There is plenty of evidence for etymological guesswork in the variant spellings recorded in the OED [Oxford English Dictionary]. Suppose you are writing about life at sea and find that a favourite dish of working seamen was called /bɜːˈguː/. If you think that this word is just nautical slang, you will spell it *burgoo*. But if you think, perhaps because of the final stress, that it may have something to do with French cooking, you will look for possible French elements and spell it *burgout*, presumably on analogy with *ragout*.
>
> (Carney, 1994:468)

For Malay, the picture is much simpler. Only the first type of awareness above (phonological awareness) is necessary. That is, if speakers know the pronunciation of a Malay word, and can segment it into syllables and constituent sounds, and know the sound-to-spelling correspondences, then they can predict with virtually 100% certainty the spelling of the word. And vice versa, given the spelling, they can predict the pronunciation. There is no need to analyse the word morphemically, or to know the historical origin of the word, or learn it visually by rote.

As a result of the simplicity of Malay spelling, teachers of Malay do not spend hours of classroom time on spelling lessons, that is instruction in the above types of awareness. Malay spelling is taught in a similar way to the spelling of Arabic, a language which has a substantial influence on Malay. Words are broken down into their constituent syllables, and those syllables into their constituent letters/sounds. Thus a word like *baring* ('lie down') is taught as <b>/b/ + <a>/a/ = /ba/; <r>/r/ + <i>/i/ + <ng>/ŋ/ = /riŋ/.

Since spelling can be taught phonically, such instruction can be got out of the way at an early stage, so that attention can be paid to more important language matters. The following episode illustrates the same point with regard to Spanish, which also has a good sound-to-spelling correspondence.

> An American professor, Edward Rondthaler, related that his grandson who lived in Mexico had just started to learn Spanish. Since the professor was interested in spelling, he asked the boy what Spanish spelling lessons were like. The boy didn't seem to understand the question. 'Well, how did you learn to spell Spanish?' Rondthaler asked. 'In the first lesson,' his grandson replied, 'the teacher wrote up the letters of the alphabet and told us what sound they each represented. Then we got on with learning the language.'
>
> (Brown, 1996:23)

Since Malay spelling can be learnt in such a simple fashion, there are no books on Malay spelling. There are certainly no equivalents of the 'Spelling made simple' books that abound for English spelling. The book *Daftar Ejaan Rumi Bahasa Malaysia (Register of Roman Alphabet Spelling for Malay)* is issued by the Dewan Bahasa dan Pustaka (Language and Literature Agency), but no further books are needed beyond this.

In Malay educational circles, no learners without psychological problems are labelled as 'poor spellers'. Also, in Malay, it is not difficult to label spellings 'right' or 'wrong'. A spelling is wrong because such a spelling could never represent the intended pronunciation. However, in English, wrong spellings may be more regular than the right spellings. Can one really say that Winnie-the-Pooh's spelling of *honey* as *hunny is* 'wrong'? *Hunny* conforms to the generalisations that *u* regularly represents /ʌ/, and that consonant letters like *n* must be doubled in order to show that the preceding vowel is short (cf *runny* vs *puny).* The only word that patterns like *honey* is *money,* whereas *hunny* resembles *bunny, funny, runny* and *sunny.*

Tasks such as those contained in this book can be used (with adaptation) for increasing phonological awareness among those learning the English spelling system (either native children or foreign learners). In this way, they can be helped with dividing words into syllables, dividing syllables into onset and rhyme (peak + coda), identifying the individual sounds in onset, peak and coda positions, and so on.

In Chapter 1, we noted that there are three phenomena that need to be kept separate:

- the written form of the letter
- the corresponding sound that the letter usually has
- the name given to the letter

We also noted that many language professionals fail to keep them distinct.

It is unavoidable that the names of letters of the alphabet need to be used, as that is how we learn the alphabet (A for *apple*, B for *bear*, etc) and spell words ('*choir* is spelt /siː eɪtʃ əʊ aɪ ɑː/'). However, they may be an obstruction for learners who equate them with the sound the letter makes. For example, it is not uncommon for children to misspell a word like *car* as *cr*. At first glance, this looks like the child has simply missed out the vowel letter *a*. However, a deeper process may be at work. The child's thinking is that *c* represents /k/, and that the letter *r* is pronounced /ɑː/. Put them together, and you get /kɑː/! Of course, the problem is that the child is mixing up the sound the letter usually has (*c* represents /k/) with the name of the letter (*r* is pronounced /ɑː/).

Spelling reform

Readers will have realised that English phonemic transcription is a response to a problem. However, as with many responses, it addresses the symptoms rather than the underlying root cause. The main problem underlying the difficulty of English spelling is that pronunciation has changed over the centuries, whereas spelling has not (for the reasons given in Chapter 2). What was needed was changes in the spelling of English to keep pace with the changes that had taken place in the pronunciation. However, this did not happen, apart from minor changes such as the American variants introduced by Noah Webster in his *American Dictionary of the English Language* of 1828 (*color, center,* etc).

What is needed is change to bring the spelling of English more in line with the current pronunciation. The idea that the spelling system of a language is an aspect that can and should be managed may be a new idea to many English-speaking readers. It will not, however, be a new idea to many non-English readers, since, as the following table shows, spelling reforms have taken place in many other major world languages.

Table 9.1: Some spelling reforms in languages

1612	Italian	1917	Norwegian
1735	French	1917	Russian
1815	Dutch	1928	Turkish
1815	Spanish	1934	Dutch
1835	French	1946	Japanese
1860	Romanian	1948	Danish
1878	French	early 1950s	Czech
1901	German	1954	Dutch
1904	Romanian	1957	Irish
1906–7	Swedish	1956	Mainland Chinese
1907	Norwegian	1959	Spanish
1909	Albanian	1972	Malay/Indonesian
1909	Norwegian	1982	Greek
1912	Brazilian Portuguese	1990	French
1915	Portugal Portuguese	1996	German

Updating the spelling system of a language by conscious management has educational benefits.

> Denmark and Sweden have very similar languages. ... Sweden updated its spelling in the last century. Danish spelling is still very much as Swedish used to be before it was reformed. Swedish spellers always come near the top in all international comparisons of standards of literacy, Danish spellers near the bottom.
>
> (Bell, 2001)

(Although, as can be seen from the table, Danish had a reform more recently (1948) than Swedish (1906–1907), the Swedish reform was substantial, whereas the Danish reform was not.)

As such exercises at regularising spelling involve changing speakers' and writers' habits and competence (in that proficient as well as non-proficient spellers are being asked to learn new spellings), such reforms often encounter resistance. The term *spelling reform* has thus come to acquire with the general public negative connotations of absent-minded professors proposing wholesale reforms of the system with the introduction of exotic letters and patterns which are a far departure from current orthography. In fact, modern proposals represent modest changes to traditional orthography by the elimination of the grossest irregularities. Reformers thus use terms like *regularised spelling* (making reference to the undeniable fact that English spelling is in many respects very irregular), *simplified spelling* (designed to eliminate the difficulties which are a barrier to learners, whether native children or foreigners), and *improved spelling* (implying that there is ample room for improvement).

Crystal (1995:276) divides spelling reform approaches into four categories:

- **Supplanting** approaches replace all existing letters by new symbols.
- **Augmenting** approaches add new symbols (diacritics and invented letters) to existing letters.
- **Standardising** approaches use familiar letters more regularly, typically by adding new two-letter combinations. No new symbols are added.
- **Regularising** approaches apply existing rules more consistently.

I have organised the approaches above in terms of the amount of departure from existing spelling symbols and rules. Given the resistance to changes in spelling by the general public, those approaches that depart most from current practices (*supplanting* and *augmenting*) are likely to be less successful than those that cause the least disruption (*standardising* and *regularising*).

The management of spelling by reform is the only way in which spelling is kept up-to-date with pronunciation, to alleviate spelling problems for learners. Such an exercise was carried out for Malay in 1972 (Asmah, 1989) following similar exercises in 1904, 1924, 1956 and 1959. As a result, Malay spelling looks like a neatly tended garden, in contrast to the unkempt jungle that is English spelling.

The main reasons why such reforms could be made in Malay and were so successful are twofold. Firstly, Malay is spoken in a small geographical area. Secondly, there is a governing body for Malay, the Dewan Bahasa dan Pustaka (and predecessor institutions). In contrast, English is spoken in so many countries worldwide. Even within individual English-speaking countries, 'English spelling has never been officially managed. There is no recognised academy or educational agency in Britain appointed to monitor the use and development of the language, as there often is for the languages of other countries' (Carney, 1994:468). Several candidates spring to mind for English: Oxford University Press (because of their reputation for dictionaries in both

British and American circles), Cambridge University (not just for their publications, but also for their involvement in English language testing), the British Council (for their status in English language teaching circles in many countries worldwide), Microsoft (who control how we spell on computer, and publish the Encarta Dictionary). However, none has quite the reputation and the authority to be accepted as a governing body for English worldwide.

An associated exercise that must accompany such reforms is the practice of respelling loanwords to fit in with the borrowing language's spelling system, perhaps with accompanying changes in the pronunciation to fit in with the borrowing language's phonology. This is normally done in Malay, whereas it tends not to happen in English (note the problems you may have experienced in recognising/transcribing French loanwords in tasks in this book). Thus it is easy to recognise the following English loanwords which have been borrowed into Malay. Their spelling has been changed to conform with Malay spelling, and to avoid the large number of irregularities in the English spelling-to-sound correspondence for *c* described in Chapter 2: *akademi, balkoni, romantik, sen, asid, eksaiz, rok, pakej, hoki, sains, akaun, vaksin, canselor, koc, krismas, kolesterol, orkid, kalsium, sivik*. Readers may even be persuaded to agree that these Malay spellings make much more sense than the conventional 'correct' English spellings of which they are borrowings.

Conclusion

English is not a 'pure' language in any sense. In terms of its history, we have seen in Chapter 2 that it is fundamentally Germanic (Anglo-Saxon), but that it has been heavily influenced at various stages by Latin, French and Old Norse. It has also borrowed many words from other languages, through the processes of colonisation and general cultural contact.

It is not a language like French, where deliberate attempts have been made to keep it 'pure'. As a result, it is hardly surprising that the English spelling system has, over the centuries, departed from the alphabetic principle on which it is based.

As explained in Chapter 2, the sequence of events – with the advent of the printing press and the resulting standardisation of spelling coming first, and the Great Vowel Shift coming second – caused standardised spellings to be out-of-date five centuries ago. The situation has not been consciously rectified in the intervening period.

If I were a Finn, Malay or Spaniard, I would not have been able to write this book, because in those languages there are no large discrepancies between spellings and pronunciations necessitating the use of phonemic symbols in dictionaries, language teaching circles, and so on. The perceptive reader will have realised that phonemic transcriptions are an attempted solution to a problem. The problem is easy to identify: the lack of anything like a one-to-one correspondence between letters and sounds in English. Indeed, English is probably the worst example of a language with a spelling system based on the alphabetic principle.

The solution – or the question of whether phonemic transcription is the solution – is more contentious. Like many so-called solutions, phonemic transcription addresses the symptoms, but does not solve the root cause of the problem. It is a kind of stopgap. The root cause is the poor sound-to-spelling and spelling-to-sound correspondences in English. Only measures taken to increase the correspondence can ultimately solve the problem – measures that have been taken for everyone's benefit in other languages.

Comparable measures have been taken in other fields. I remember, as a child growing up in Britain, the difficulties of dealing with money before decimalisation in 1971. A pound was divided into 20 shillings, and each shilling had 12 pence. You can imagine the complexity of school maths questions that took the form 'If I buy seven articles at £1 3s 5d each, how much change will I have from a £10 note?' Things became much easier after the currency became more regular through decimalisation, which uses the base ten. Systems for weights are going through the same sort of regularisation. In Britain, I would say that my weight was 11½ stone. When I left Britain, I soon changed that to 161 lbs (there are 14 lbs in a stone), thereby getting rid of the non-decimal stone unit. I am nowadays more comfortable with 70 kg, in the truly decimal system (there are 2.2 lbs to the kilogram). I now take decimal money and weight measures for granted, and am glad I no longer talk about shillings and stones. I wonder whether, in centuries to come, people will look back and shake their heads in disbelief at the irregular spelling system currently used for English.

In a more philosophical vein, we might consider what we feel the main purpose of a spelling system is. Some would emphasise the function of English spelling as a reflection of the historical development of the language. Others would argue that the status quo is acceptable – that they personally have no intention of sanctioning changes in English spelling, since they have invested so much time and effort into mastering it in the first place, even if this means that illiterate individuals who, for whatever reason, have never mastered it, continue to be disadvantaged. To my mind, the function of a spelling system is primarily to allow all users, whether proficient adults, children learning the language or foreign learners, to decode easily when reading, and encode easily when writing. At present, the English spelling system does not allow that. As the Simplified Spelling Society website notes, 'neglect of the alphabetic principle now makes literacy unnecessarily difficult in English throughout the world, and learning, education and communication all suffer.' As a result, phonemic transcription is at present a necessary evil.

Answer keys

Task 1.1 Searching for sound types (page 8) 

A The following words begin with a plosive sound:

blossom /blɒsəm/
business /bɪznɪs/
chasm /kæzəm/ [1]
Christmas /krɪsməs/ [1]
counter /kaʊntə/
distinct /dɪstɪŋkt/
dressmaker /dresmeɪkə/
grocer /grəʊsə/
kiss /kɪs/
penknife /pennaɪf/
playground /pleɪgraʊnd/
pterodactyl /terədæktɪl/ [2]
quiche /kiːʃ/ [3]
quick /kwɪk/ [4]
tackle /tækəl/
thyme /taɪm/ [5]
twenty /twenti/

1 *ch* = /k/ here, Greek origin
2 initial /t/, not /p/, 'silent' *p*, Greek origin
3 *qu* = /k/ here, French origin
4 *qu* = /kw/ here
5 *th* = /t/ here

The following words do not begin with a plosive sound:

chalet /ʃæleɪ/ (*ch* = /ʃ/ here, French origin)
chase /tʃeɪs/ (/tʃ/ is an affricate, not a plosive)
gentleman /dʒentəlmən/ (/dʒ/ is an affricate, not a plosive)
gnaw /nɔː/ ('silent' *g*)
GMT /dʒiː em tiː/ (Note the pronunciation of the name of the letter G)
phonetics /fənetɪks/ (*ph* = /f/ here, Greek origin)
pneumatic /njuːmætɪk/ ('silent' *p*, Greek origin)
therapeutic /θerəpjuːtɪk/ (*th* = /θ/ here)

B The following words end with a plosive sound:

arctic /ɑːktɪk/
aside /əsaɪd/
big /bɪg/
board /bɔːd/
bribe /braɪb/
debate /dɪbeɪt/
invent /ɪnvent/
jump /dʒʌmp/
kerb /kɜːb/
look /lʊk/
monarch /mɒnək/
rebuke /rɪbjuːk/
restaurant /restərɒnt/ [1]
returned /rɪtɜːnd/
rope /rəʊp/
scratched /skrætʃt/
shirt /ʃɜːt/
sleep /sliːp/
trick /trɪk/

1 This is the typical English pronunciation of this French word. The *Longman Pronunciation Dictionary* also gives /-rɒŋ/ (ie with a final syllable pronounced as *wrong*) and /-rɒ̃, -rɑ̃ː, -rɔ̃ː/ (ie with nasalised vowels, as in the original French).

The following words do not end with a plosive sound:
arch /ɑːtʃ/ (but /ɑːk/ in *archangel*)
ballet /bæleɪ/ ('silent' *t*, French origin)
GMT /dʒiː em tiː/ (Note the pronunciation of the name of the letter *T*)
limb /lɪm/ ('silent' *b*)
marriage /mærɪdʒ/
string /strɪŋ/ (*ng* = /ŋ/ here)

C The following words begin with a fricative sound:

chic /ʃiːk/ [1]
fuss /fʌs/
genre /ʒɒnrə/ [2]
hippo /hɪpəʊ/
philosophy /fɪlɒsəfi/
sheep /ʃiːp/
sugar /ʃʊgə/
Susan /suːzən/
there /ðeə/
thick /θɪk/
very /veri/
VIP /viː aɪ piː/ [3]
zinc /zɪŋk/

1 *ch* = /ʃ/ here, French origin
2 French origin
3 Note the pronunciation of the name of the letter *V*

The following words do not begin with a fricative sound:
cello /tʃeləʊ/ (*ch* = /tʃ/ here, Italian origin)
chick /tʃɪk/ (/tʃ/ is an affricate, not a fricative)
FM /ef em/ (Note the pronunciation of the name of the letter *F*)
H_2O /eɪtʃ tuː əʊ/ (Note the pronunciation of the name of the letter *H*. The *Longman Pronunciation Dictionary* states that the

pronunciation /heɪtʃ/ is standard in Irish English, but not in British or American English.)

honour /ɒnə/ ('silent' *h*)

SOB /es əʊ biː/ (Note that the name of the oil company Esso is a representation of the letters *SO*, for Standard Oil)

Thomas /tɒməs/ (*th* = /t/ here. The only other common words where *th* = /t/ are *Anthony, Esther, Lesotho, Thailand, Thames, Theresa, thyme*)

D The following words end with a fricative sound:

barrage /bærɑːʒ/ [1]	*jazz* /dʒæz/	*quiche* /kiːʃ/
breathe /briːð/	*lease* /liːs/	*race* /reɪs/
chase /tʃeɪs/	*loch* /lɒx/ [3]	*rocks* /rɒks/
cough /kɒf/	*of* /ɒv/ [2]	*save* /seɪv/
eggs /egz/	*off* /ɒf/	*size* /saɪz/
fish /fɪʃ/	*Paris* /pærɪs/ [4]	*triumph* /traɪʌmf/
fox /fɒks/	*path* /pɑːθ/	*with* /wɪð/ [2]
giraffe /dʒɪrɑːf/	*please* /pliːz/ [5]	
is /ɪz/ [2]	*quartz* /kwɔːts/ [6]	

1 If this French word is not pronounced with final /dʒ/ (see syllable structure rules, Chapter 6).

2 Note that the three common words *is, of* and *with* have unexpectedly voiced final consonants.

3 If this Gaelic word is not pronounced with final /k/ (see Chapter 2, on spelling-to-sound correspondence for *c*).

4 This is the English pronunciation of this French placename. In French, it has no final fricative /s/.

5 Notice, from the pronunciation of *lease* and *please*, that the spelling is generally not a good indicator between voiced and voiceless final consonants.

6 A German loanword.

The following words do not end with a fricative sound:

chassis /ʃæsi/	*grand prix* /grɒn priː/	*watch* /wɒtʃ/
cheetah /tʃiːtə/	*laissez (-faire)* /leɪseɪ feə/	

Chassis, grand prix and *laissez-faire* are all of French origin. French has many 'silent' final consonant letters.

E The following words begin with a nasal sound:

gnome /nəʊm/ [1]	*Mr* /mɪstə/
knowledge /nɒlɪdʒ/ [2]	*NASA* /næsə/ [4]
mimic /mɪmɪk/	*naughty* /nɔːti/
mnemonic /nɪmɒnɪk/ [3]	*pneumonia* /njuːməʊniə/ [5]

1 'Silent' *g*
2 'Silent' *k*
3 Note the initial /n/, 'silent' *m*
4 Note this is not pronounced as initials /en eɪ es eɪ/
5 'Silent' *p*

The following words do not begin with a nasal sound:
MTV /em tiː viː/
NEC /en iː siː/

F The following words end with a consonant sound:

banquet /bæŋkwɪt/	*garage* /gærɑːʒ/ [1]	*thumb* /θʌm/ [3]
complete /kəmpliːt/	*panache* /pənæʃ/ [2]	

1 Final /dʒ/ for some speakers, French origin
2 French origin
3 'Silent' *b*

The following words do not end with a consonant sound:

debris /deɪbriː/ [1]	*happy* /hæpi/	*square* /skweə/
deny /dɪnaɪ/	*parquet* /pɑːkeɪ/ [1]	*stranger* /streɪndʒə/
draw /drɔː/	*pillow* /pɪləʊ/	
four /fɔː/	*rendezvous* /rɒndeɪvuː/ [1]	

1 French origin

Task 1.2 Searching for /j/ words (pages 9 and 10)

The correct route is:

beauty	/bjuːti/	*yellow*	/jeləʊ/
UK	/juː keɪ/	*Q&A*	/kjuː ənd eɪ/
yacht	/jɒt/	*unit*	/juːnɪt/
Uruguay	/jʊərəgwaɪ/	*youth*	/juːθ/
few	/fjuː/	*cute*	/kjuːt/
useful	/juːsfʊl/	*W*	/dʌbəl juː/
Europe	/jʊərəp/		

This task, and Tasks 1.3, 1.7, 1.9, 4.6 and 6.4 all involve searching for particular sounds or features. It is much more motivating and fun for the students if the tasks are made into a game, rather than tasks of the 'Tick which words contain /j/' type. This format can be used for any sounds or features that your students have problems with. Use one of the above formats, plot the correct route and put in the appropriate words, and then fill in the rest with distractors.

Task 1.3 Searching for /g/ words (pages 9 and 11)

The correct route is:

gift	/gɪft/	*single*	/sɪŋgəl/
anger	/æŋgə/	*guess*	/ges/
guard	/gɑːd/	*gum*	/gʌm/
gold	/gəʊld/	*drag*	/dræg/
frog	/frɒg/	*gave*	/geɪv/
ghastly	/gɑːsli/	*ghost*	/gəʊst/

Task 1.4 Transcription to spelling 1 (page 19)

whose	*comb*	*juice*	*young*
calm	*shove*	*flood*	*liquor*
deaf	*debt*	*Thames*	*occur*
ache	*friend*	*tomb*	*honour*
prayer	*breast*	*could*	*pretty*

Task 1.5 *Peter eats cheese in Greece* (page 19)

Possible words are:

	Name	Food	Country	Sport	Car
/g/	*Gordon*	*eggs*	*Mongolia*	*rugby*	*Lamborghini*
/ɒ/	*Jonathan*	*sausages*	*Australia*	*squash*	*Honda*

Task 1.6 Transcription to spelling 2 (page 20)

height	*yacht*	*break, brake*	*women*
psalm	*gnome*	*mousse, moose*	*cupboard*
weird	*ghoul*	*figure*	*wrestle*
knack	*rhyme*	*cousin*	*column*
heart	*wheeze*	*Buddha*	*plumber*

Task 1.7 Searching for /e/ words (pages 20 and 21)

The correct route is:

web	/web/	*chess*	/tʃes/
leisure	/leʒə/	*well*	/wel/
head	/hed/	*deaf*	/def/
many	/meni/	*speck*	/spek/
debt	/det/	*leopard*	/lepəd/
breath	/breθ/	*friend*	/frend/
bed	/bed/	*bury*	/beri/
any	/eni/	*centre*	/sentə/

Task 1.8 Transcription to spelling 3 (page 22)

crèche	*brochure*	*ginger*	*lasso*
scarce	*design*	*clumsy*	*bosom*
pizza	*canoe*	*bouquet*	*reservoir*
acquit	*cuisine*	*scissors*	*unique*
lacquer	*panicked*	*flourish*	*century*

Task 1.9 Searching for /ɑː/ words (pages 22 and 23) 

The correct route is:

star	/stɑː/	*laugh*	/lɑːf/
half	/hɑːf/	*heart*	/hɑːt/
almond	/ɑːmənd/	*shark*	/ʃɑːk/
hard	/hɑːd/	*drama*	/drɑːmə/
clerk	/klɑːk/	*palm*	/pɑːm/
father	/fɑːðə/	*dance*	/dɑːns/
charm	/tʃɑːm/	*pass*	/pɑːs/

Task 1.10 Transcription to spelling 4 (page 22) 

scythe	*writhe*	*exhaust*	*vicious*
waltz	*sachet, sashay*	*seizure*	*squalid*
sphinx	*sovereign*	*champagne*	*repertoire*
brooch, broach	*psycho*	*Nazi*	*courtesy*
scourge	*cliché*	*knowledge*	*knuckle*

Task 1.11 Sound anagrams (page 24) 

Rover /rəʊvə/	*Honda* /hɒndə/
Ford /fɔːd/	*Lotus* /ləʊtəs/
Volvo /vɒlvəʊ/	*Renault* /renəʊ/
Porsche /pɔːʃ/	*Chrysler* /kraɪzlə/
Mazda /mæzdə/	*Toyota* /tɔɪəʊtə/
Opel /əʊpəl/	*Chevrolet* /ʃevrəleɪ/

Tasks such as this one are easy to create, and can be used to practice particular sounds and words that your students have problems with. However, a clue should be given as to what the students are looking for. In this task, it is names of cars. In Tasks 6.7 and 7.4, definitions of the search items are given. In Task 7.6, famous people's surnames are given.

Task 1.12 Transcription to spelling 5 (page 24) 

phlegm	*toupée*	*diaphragm*	*euphoric*
chateau	*Xerox*	*chauffeur*	*silhouette*
colonel, kernel	*fuchsia*	*attorney*	*complexion*
bureau	*caffeine*	*protégé*	*Belgian*
turquoise	*noxious*	*millionaire*	*nougat*

Task 1.13 Identifying transcription errors (page 25)

Here is the correct transcription, with the error underlined.

Russia	/<u>r</u>ʌʃə/ [1]	*maximum*	/mæ<u>ks</u>ɪməm/
compare	/kəmp<u>eə</u>/	*chief*	/tʃ<u>iː</u>f/
ninth	/naɪn<u>θ</u>/	*whisker*	/<u>wɪ</u>skə/
quicksand	/<u>kw</u>ɪksænd/	*paragraph*	/pærəgrɑː<u>f</u>/
yesterday	/<u>j</u>estədeɪ/	*utensil*	/<u>j</u>uːtensəl/
splash	/splæ<u>ʃ</u>/	*Hannah*	/hæn<u>ə</u>/
rainfall	/r<u>eɪ</u>nfɔːl/	*airport*	/eəp<u>ɔː</u>t/
custard	/<u>k</u>ʌstəd/	*Finnish*	/fɪ<u>n</u>ɪʃ/ [2]
anything	/<u>e</u>nɪθɪŋ/	*uncle*	/ʌ<u>ŋ</u>kəl/
javelin	/<u>dʒ</u>ævlɪn/	*Thailand*	/<u>t</u>aɪlænd/
archer	/ɑː<u>tʃ</u>ə/	*infer*	/ɪnf<u>ɜː</u>/
fertile	/f<u>ɜːt</u>aɪl/	*homemade*	/həʊ<u>mm</u>eɪd/ [2]

1 None of the phonemic symbols for English looks like a capital. Capitalisation is a spelling phenomenon. Thus, *Russia* and *rusher* are both /rʌʃə/.

2 There is only one /n/ sound in *Finnish*; it is thus the same as *finish*. However, there are two /m/s (pronounced as one double-length /m/) in *homemade*.

Task 1.14 Names of letters of the alphabet (page 26)

/e/	/iː/	/eɪ/	/uː/	Others
F /ef/ L /el/ M /em/ N /en/ S /es/ X /eks/ Z /zed/ [1]	B /biː/ C /siː/ D /diː/ E /iː/ G /dʒiː/ P /piː/ T /tiː/ V /viː/	A /eɪ/ H /eɪtʃ/ J /dʒeɪ/ K /keɪ/	Q /kjuː/ U /juː/ W /dʌbəl juː/	I /aɪ/ O /əʊ/ R /ɑː(r)/ Y /waɪ/

1 Americans pronounce Z /zed/ as /ziː/, ie with the vowel of B, C, D, etc.

Task 1.15 Initialisms (page 26)

ATM	/eɪ tiː em/	OBE	/əʊ biː iː/
BMW	/biː em dʌbəl juː/	POW	/piː əʊ dʌbəl juː/
DVD	/diː viː diː/	RSVP	/ɑːr es viː piː/
HRD	/eɪtʃ ɑː diː/	SUV	/es juː viː/
ICBM	/aɪ siː biː em/	UFO	/juː ef əʊ/
LCD	/el siː diː/	VIP	/viː aɪ piː/
MSc	/em es siː/	YMCA	/waɪ em siː eɪ/

Task 1.16 *A* or *an*? (page 27)

The rule should be phrased: '*An*, rather than *a*, occurs before any vowel sound'. Conversely, *a* occurs before any consonant sound. Thus, we say *an MSc* /ən em es siː/ because the pronunciation of MSc begins with the /e/ vowel, regardless of the fact that M might be considered a consonant letter. Conversely, we say *a UFO* /ə juː ef əʊ/ because the pronunciation of U begins with the /j/ consonant, even though U might be considered a vowel letter. In short, this rule depends on the pronunciation; the spelling is irrelevant.

Be wary of English spelling 'rules' that you may have heard, such as '*i* before *e* except after *c*', or 'If a noun or verb ends in *y*, make it an *i* before adding the *-es* or *-ed* ending'. Most such rules are usually at best tendencies (ie there are many exceptions) or rules that are over-stated and need some refinement. The first was devised to account for words such as *field, receive,* but fails to account for many others (*weird, neighbour* and, conversely, *science, ancient,* etc). Similarly, the second accounts for *tries, fancies* (which, of course, contradicts the first rule just stated!) but not for *delays, monkeys, boys,* etc. In short, neither rule is as simple as most people state them to be. And the same is true of '*An,* not *a,* occurs before *a, e, i, o* or *u*'.

Task 1.17 Words that are names of letters of the alphabet (page 27)

A	*a* [1]	J	*jay*	R	*are* [1]
B	*bee, be* [1]	O	*owe*	T	*tea, tee*
C	*see, sea*	P	*pea, pee*	U	*you, yew, ewe*
I	*I, eye, aye*	Q	*queue, cue, Kew* [2]	Y	*why*

1 If *a, be* and *are* are pronounced as full strong forms, then they are /eɪ, biː, ɑː/, ie the same as the letters A, B and R. However, they are usually weakened in connected speech to /ə, bɪ, ə/ (see Chapter 5).
2 A district of London, famous for its botanical gardens.

Some letters are pronounced the same as names. For instance, the girl's name Kay is pronounced the same as the letter K. There is a river in north Wales, and another in east Scotland call the River Dee, pronounced the same as the letter D.

The names of some of these letters have the same pronunciation as common exclamations. Thus, *eh?, ee!, gee!, oh!* and *ah!* have the same pronunciation as the letters A, E, G, O and R.

A curious internet example is ICQ, where the pronunciation /aɪ siː kjuː/ is the same as *I seek you* /aɪ siːk juː/, provided the /k/ sound is assumed to link to the next word.

Task 2.1 Guessing from spelling (page 41) 

The basic problem here is that there are no regular correspondence patterns for the *-ough-* spelling. If you think that *chough* is like *cough,* you will guess it is pronounced /tʃɒf/. If like *bough,* then /tʃaʊ/. If like *through,* then /tʃuː/. And so on. In fact, *chough* patterns like *enough,* and is pronounced /tʃʌf/.

The following answers are given in the *Longman Pronunciation Dictionary*:

brougham /bruːəm/ or /bruːm/ (that is, it resembles *through*)
chough /tʃʌf/ (resembling *enough*)
clough /klʌf/ (resembling *enough*)

doughty /daʊti/ (resembling *bough*)
hough /hɒk/ (as if it were spelt *hock*)
slough (noun) 'muddy ground' /slaʊ/ (resembling *bough*), AmE /sluː/ (resembling *through*). The *Longman Pronunciation Dictionary* notes that 'some Americans make a distinction between /sluː/ in the literal sense and /slaʊ/ in the figurative', for example *slough of despond*.
(verb) (eg of a snake) 'to shed skin' /slʌf/ (resembling *enough*).
sough /saʊ/ or /sʌf/ (resembling *bough* or *enough*)

The problems are even worse if we consider surnames and place names. Look up the following in the *Longman Pronunciation Dictionary*. Note that some have variant pronunciations, and that some place names are pronounced differently in different parts of the UK.

Bough, Broughton, Coughton, Gough, Loughborough, Poughill, Stoughton, Troughton

Task 2.2 'Silent' letters 1 (page 43) 

The only two letters of the alphabet that seem never to be 'silent' are *j* and *v*. That is, they always represent some sound. Here is one 'silent' example of each the other 24 letters (underlined):

A: *bread* /bred/
B: *debt* /det/
C: *science* /saɪəns/
D: *handsome* /hænsəm/
E: *height* /haɪt/
F: *halfpenny* /heɪpni/
G: *gnaw* /nɔː/
H: *whales* /weɪlz/ [1]
I: *friend* /frend/
K: *knew* /njuː/
L: *salmon* /sæmən/
M: *mnemonic* /nɪmɒnɪk/
N: *autumn* /ɔːtəm/
O: *young* /jʌŋ/
P: *psychology* /saɪkɒlədʒi/
Q: *racquet* /rækɪt/ [2]
R: *Worcester* /wʊstə/
S: *island* /aɪlənd/
T: *mortgage* /mɔːgɪdʒ/
U: *build* /bɪld/
W: *wring* /rɪŋ/
X: *grand prix* /priː/
Y: *key* /kiː/
Z: *rendezvous* /rɒndeɪvuː/

1 Some speakers make a distinction between *whales* /hweɪlz/ and *Wales* /weɪlz/.
2 An alternative spelling for *racket*.

Task 2.3 'Silent' letters 2 (page 43)

autumn inert, because of the related adjective *autumnal* /ɔːtʌmnəl/
bomb inert, because of the related verb *bombard* /bɒmbɑːd/
Christmas empty
country empty (it is not related to *county*)
debt empty
doubt empty
dumb empty
give empty (the *e* does not work with the letter *i* to give /aɪ/ as in *five* /faɪv/)
hasten inert, because of the word *haste* /heɪst/
hate auxiliary (the *e* works with the letter *a* to give /eɪ/)
isle empty
lamb empty
phlegm inert, because of the adjective *phlegmatic* /flegmætɪk/
receipt inert, because of the related words *reception, recipient, receptacle*
shelf auxiliary (the *h* works with the letter *s* to give /ʃ/)
two inert, because of the related words *twice, twelve, twenty, twin*

Task 3.1 Providing consonant minimal pairs (page 49)

Possible answers (there are many other examples for each permutation):

	/p/	/s/	/w/
/k/	*coke, cop* /kəʊk, kəʊp/	*cake, sake* /keɪk, seɪk/ *break, brace* /breɪk, breɪs/	*chord, ward* /kɔːd, wɔːd/
/m/	*mine, pine* /maɪn, paɪn/ *hymn, hip* /hɪm, hɪp/	*mix, six* /mɪks, sɪks/ *rhyme, rice* /raɪm, raɪs/	*mall, wall* /mɔːl, wɔːl/
/tʃ/	*cheap, peep* /tʃiːp, piːp/ *match, map* /mætʃ, mæp/	*chew, sue* /tʃuː, suː/ *perch, purse* /pɜːtʃ, pɜːs/	*cheat, wheat* /tʃiːt, wiːt/

Note that /w/ does not occur syllable-finally: see syllable structure rules, Chapter 6.

Task 3.2 Providing vowel minimal pairs (page 50)

Possible answers (there are many other examples for each permutation):

	/iː/	/uː/	/aʊ/
/æ/	*sat, seat* /sæt, siːt/	*flat, flute* /flæt, fluːt/	*band, bound* /bænd, baʊnd/
/ɒ/	*shop, sheep* /ʃɒp, ʃiːp/	*hot, hoot* /hɒt, huːt/	*moss, mouse* /mɒs, maʊs/
/əʊ/	*foal, feel* /fəʊl, fiːl/	*show, shoe* /ʃəʊ, ʃuː/	*groaned, ground* /grəʊnd, graʊnd/

Task 3.3 Identifying minimal pairs (page 50) 

cell, Seoul	Minimal pair for /e, əʊ/ (/sel, səʊl/)
chef, shed	Minimal pair for /f, d/ (/ʃef, ʃed/)
choirs, quires	Homophones (/kwaɪəz/)
dent, daren't	Minimal pair for /e, eə/ (/dent, deənt/)
fuchsias, futures	Minimal pair for /ʃ, tʃ/ (/fjuːʃəz, fjuːtʃəz/)
germs, James	Minimal pair for /ɜː, eɪ/ (/dʒɜːmz, dʒeɪmz/)
ghost, host	Minimal pair for /g, h/ (/gəʊst, həʊst/)
grape, graph	Not a minimal pair (/greɪp, grɑːf/)
liquor, liver	Minimal pair for /k, v/ (/lɪkə, lɪvə/)
mesh, mess	Minimal pair for /ʃ, s/ (/meʃ, mes/)
model, muddle	Minimal pair for /ɒ, ʌ/ (/mɒdəl, mʌdəl/)
peer, pier	Homophones (/pɪə/)
phone, prone	Not a minimal pair (/fəʊn, prəʊn/)
sing, sink	Not a minimal pair (/sɪŋ, sɪŋk/)
though, trough	Not a minimal pair (/ðəʊ, trɒf/)
tomb, room	Minimal pair for /t, r/ (/tuːm, ruːm/)
wealth, Welsh	Minimal pair for /θ, ʃ/ (/welθ, welʃ/)
which, witch	Homophones (/wɪtʃ/)

Task 3.4 Frames for minimal pairs (page 51)

The following are existing words. Look them up in a dictionary, if necessary:

	/h __ d/	/b __ /	/f __ z/	/s __ t/	/p __ l/
/iː/	*heed*	*be, bee*	*fees*	*seat*	*peel, peal*
/ɪ/	*hid*		*fizz*	*sit*	*pill*
/e/	*head*		*fez*	*set*	*pell(-mell)*
/æ/	*had*			*sat*	*pal*
/ʌ/			*fuzz*		
/ɑː/	*hard*	*bar*			
/ɒ/	*hod*			*sot*	
/ɔː/	*hoard, horde*	*bore, boar*	*fours*	*sort, sought*	*Paul, pall*
/ʊ/	*hood*			*soot*	*pull*
/uː/	*who'd*	*boo*		*suit*	*pool*
/ɜː/	*heard*	*burr*	*furs, firs*	*cert*	*pearl, purl*
/eɪ/		*bay*	*phase, faze*	*sate*	*pail, pale*
/aɪ/	*hide*	*buy*		*site, cite, sight*	*pile*
/ɔɪ/		*boy*			
/aʊ/		*bow, bough*			*Powell*
/əʊ/	*hoed*	*(rain)bow*	*foes*		*pole, poll*
/ɪə/		*beer*	*fears*		
/eə/	*haired*	*bare, bear*	*fares, fairs*		
/ʊə/		*boor*			

Note that all the entries for /b __ / involve long vowels (see syllable structure rules, Chapter 6).

Task 4.1 Identifying homophones (page 54)

/kiː/ *key, quay*
/dʒɪm/ *Jim, gym*
/weɪst/ *waste, waist*
/ʃuːt/ *shoot, chute*
/reks/ *Rex, wrecks*
/grəʊn/ *groan, grown*
/siːlɪŋ/ *sealing, ceiling*
/nəʊz/ *nose, knows*
/biːtəl/ *beetle, betel* (and *Beatle*[1])
/kjuː/ *cue, queue, Q* (and *Kew*[2])
/sent/ *sent, cent, scent*
/reɪn/ *rain, rein, reign*

/waɪnd/ *wind, wined, whined*
/preɪz/ *prays, praise, preys*
/tʃek/ *check, cheque*[3], *Czech*
/maɪnə/ *miner, minor, myna(h)*
/weɪ/ *way, weigh, whey*
/raɪt/ *right, write, rite, wright*[4]
/siːz/ *sees, seas, seize, Cs*
/mɑːk/ *mark, Mark, marque, mach*
/piːk/ *peak, peek, pique, peke*[5]
/eə/ *air, heir, ere*[6], *e'er*[7], *Ayr*[8], *Eyre*[9]

1 For example *John Lennon was a Beatle*
2 A district of London, famous for its botanical gardens
3 Americans spell this *check,* ie the same as *check* (= 'inspect')
4 As in *playwright,* or as a surname (*Wright*)
5 An abbreviation for *Pekinese* dog
6 A poetic word meaning 'before'
7 A poetic version of *ever*
8 A town in Scotland
9 As in *Jane Eyre* by Charlotte Bronte

Task 4.2 Identifying homographs (page 55)

bow	/bəʊ, baʊ/	*bass*	/beɪs, bæs/
live	/lɪv, laɪv/	*close*	/kləʊs, kləʊz/
read	/riːd, red/	*sow*	/səʊ, saʊ/
wound	/wuːnd, waʊnd/	*routed*	/ruːtɪd, raʊtɪd/
use	/juːs, juːz/	*putting*	/pʊtɪŋ, pʌtɪŋ/
tear	/tɪə, teə/		

The following example involves a difference in the number of syllables:
aged /eɪdʒd, eɪdʒɪd/

The following examples involve differences in stress placement:

minute	/'mɪnɪt, maɪ'njuːt/	*content*	/'kɒntent, kən'tent/
invalid	/'ɪnvəlɪd, ɪn'vælɪd/	*deserts*	/'dezəts, dɪ'zɜːts/
entrance	/'entrəns, ɪn'trɑːns/		

Task 4.3 Identifying homographs and homonyms in jokes (page 57)

Homophones

/faʊl/: *foul* 'something against the rules' and *fowl* 'chicken'
/naɪts/: *knights* 'medieval soldiers' and *nights* 'hours of darkness'
/fɑːðə/: *father* 'male parent' and *farther* 'more far'
/sɪəriəl/: *cereal* 'breakfast food' and *serial* 'story in instalments'
/nʌn/: *none* 'not any' and *nun* 'female monk'
/raɪts/: *rights* 'opposite of *wrongs*' and *Wrights* 'the Wright brothers'
/prɒfɪt/: *profit* 'financial surplus' and *prophet* 'religious leader'
/peəz/: *pairs* 'couples' and *pears* 'fruit'
/ɑːk/: *ark* 'wooden boat' and *Arc* 'place in France'
/meɪd/: *made* 'constructed' and *maid* 'girl'

Homonyms

/flaɪz/: *flies* (i) 'moves through the air' (verb) and (ii) 'insects' (noun)
/laɪk/: *like* (i) 'in the manner of' (preposition) and (ii) 'enjoy' (verb)
/tæp/: *tap* (i) 'hit with the foot' and (ii) 'apparatus for controlling water flow'
/faɪn/: *fine* (i) 'OK' (adjective) and (ii) 'penalty' (noun)
/fɑːst/: *fast* (i) 'quick' (adjective) and (ii) 'abstain from eating and drinking' (verb)
/ræʃ/: *rash* (i) 'skin infection' (noun) and (ii) 'impetuous' (adjective)
/daʊn/: *down* (i) 'opposite of *up*' (adverb), and (ii) 'feathers' (noun)
/neɪlz/: *nails* (i) 'metal spikes' and (ii) as in *fingernails*
/liːn/: *lean* (i) 'not fatty' (adjective) and (ii) 'not stand upright' (verb)
/bɪl/: *bill* (i) 'invoice for payment' and (ii) 'bird's beak'
/klɪf/: (i) *Cliff* (name) and (ii) *cliff* 'steep rock'
/dʌg/: (i) *Doug* (name, short for Douglas) and (ii) *dug* (from the verb *dig*)
/maɪk/: (i) *Mike* (name, short for Michael) and (ii) *mike* (short for *microphone*)
/dʒæk/: (i) *Jack* (name, a variant of John) and (ii) *jack* 'lifting equipment'
/rɒb/: (i) *Rob* (name, short for Robert) and (ii) *rob* 'steal'
/nɪk/: (i) *Nick* (name, short for Nicholas) and (ii) *nick* (informal for 'steal')
/dʒɪm/: (i) *Jim* (name, short for James) and (ii) *gym* (short for *gymnasium*)
/wɒrən/: (i) *Warren* (name) and (ii) *warren* 'underground rabbit home'
/red/: (i) *Red* 'Russian' and (ii) *red* 'colour'
/nəʊz/: (i) *knows* and (ii) *nose*
/reɪn/: (i) *rain* and (ii) *rein*
/dɪə/: (i) *dear* and (ii) *deer*

Strictly speaking, *Red* ('Russian') and *red* ('colour') are not homonyms. They are, in fact, the same word (polysemy). They have the same historical origin. The 'Russian' sense developed from the original 'colour' sense, because the communists' flag was red. The 'colour' sense is the more basic, original, literal sense, and the 'Russian' sense is a metaphorical extension of this.

Many of the tasks in this book involve jokes, riddles, and so on. Using these has several benefits: (i) they create a good atmosphere in class, when students may be embarrassed about pronunciation, (ii) students remember them, and (iii) they show that speakers of the language (such as cartoonists) are well aware of phenomena such as homophones, and exploit them; these are not just linguistic phenomena for academics. It is worth collecting a file of riddles, cartoons cut out from newspapers and magazines.

Task 4.4 Identifying homophones and homonyms in *Alice in Wonderland* (page 59)

The plays-on-words depend on the following words:

Tale and *tail,* both /teɪl/ (homophones)
Tortoise and *taught us,* both /tɔːtəs/ (homophones)
Lesson and *lessen,* both /lesən/ (homophones)
Whiting ('fish') and *whiting* (nonce opposite of *blacking*), both /waɪtɪŋ/ (homonyms)
Soles ('fish') and *soles* ('bottoms of shoes'), both /səʊlz/ (polysemy: see note below)
Eels and *(h)eels,* both /iːlz/ (homophones)
Bark ('noise of dog') and *bark* (of tree), both /bɑːk/ (homonyms)
Bough (of *bough-wough,* nowadays more often spelt *bow-wow* 'noise of dog barking') and *bough* ('branch'), both /baʊ/ (homonyms)
Hoarse and *horse,* both /hɔːs/ (homophones)
Miss (term of address) and *miss* ('be absent'), both /mɪs/ (homonyms)
Fast (as in *stuck fast*) and *fast* ('quick'), both /fɑːst/ (homonyms)
Flour and *flower,* both /flaʊə/ (homophones)
Ground (from *grind*) and *ground* ('land'), both /graʊnd/ (homonyms)

Notes

- Since plays-on-words depend on pronunciation, and since pronunciation varies between accents, not all these plays-on-words may work in all accents. For instance, Scots pronounce *tortoise* as /tɒrtɔɪz/. It is therefore not a homophone of *taught us* for them.
- Strictly speaking, *soles* ('fish') and *soles* ('bottoms of shoes') are not homonyms. They are, in fact, polysemous, with the same historical origin. The 'bottom of shoe' sense developed from the original 'fish' sense, because they are both flat. However, most present-day speakers of English will not see this connection.
- Many plays-on-words rely on near-homophones or mispronunciations, rather than exact homophones. For instance, the *eels/heels* play-on-words only work if one accepts that the /h/ of *heels* is often dropped by some speakers.

We just said that cartoons serve useful functions in language teaching. The same can be said for extracts from literature. It need not be classic, 'high' literature, but any work that students might be encouraged to read for themselves.

Task 4.5 Searching for homophones 1 (page 61)

The corrected spellings are highlighted, and the transcriptions (which represent both the wrong and the right words) are given immediately afterwards.

Last week /wiːk/, I took my dear /dɪə/, sweet /swiːt/ little dog to the beach /biːtʃ/. We went by our usual route /ruːt/, but along the road /rəʊd/, we had to brake /breɪk/ suddenly as there /ðeə/ had been an accident. We saw /sɔː/ a car being towed /təʊd/ away.

Having been born /bɔːn/ and bred /bred/ at the seaside, I /aɪ/ always enjoy these visits, especially on a Sunday /sʌndeɪ/.

My dog, Rex /reks/, loved it. I threw /θruː/ a ball for him. Sometimes he caught /kɔːt/ it; sometimes he missed /mɪst/ it. Once he had to go into the sea /siː/ and swim against the current /kʌrənt/ to fetch a ball I had thrown /θrəʊn/ for him /hɪm/. I used to throw a piece /piːs/ of wood /wʊd/, but he always dug /dʌg/ a hole /həʊl/ in order to bury /beri/ it.

In the course /kɔːs/ of the afternoon, we went for a walk towards the naval /neɪvəl/ dockyard farther /fɑːðə/ down the beach. Near the quay /kiː/, Rex /reks/ started to wade /weɪd/ into the water and managed to find /faɪnd/ some seaweed and mussels /mʌsəlz/. He brought them to me proudly, and wagged his tail /teɪl/. But they smelt foul /faʊl/, so I had to shoo /ʃuː/ him away. We won't go near that pier /pɪə/ again.

Later, I sat on the sand to watch the tide /taɪd/ go out and the last rays /reɪz/ of the sun /sʌn/ go down below the horizon. It was one /wʌn/ of the most beautiful sights /saɪts/ I've ever seen /siːn/. But then it began to rain /reɪn/. So /səʊ/ we got in the car and made /meɪd/ our way /weɪ/ home as night /naɪt/ fell.

Notice how, in this task, you are given one of the homophones and are asked to supply the other. This is a much easier process than that in Task 4.1, of being given a transcription and being asked for homophones. If students are anxious about transcription, it makes sense to start from what they already know, that is the pronunciation of familiar words.

Task 4.6 Searching for homophones 2 (pages 61 and 62)

The correct path is formed by the following homophone pairs:

bear, bare (/beə/)	*leek, leak* (/liːk/)
ceiling, sealing (/siːlɪŋ/)	*cord, chord* (/kɔːd/)
weight, wait (/weɪt/)	*dye, die* (/daɪ/)
guessed, guest (/gest/)	*Wales, wails* (/weɪlz/)
kneel, Neil (/niːl/)	*flour, flower* (/flaʊə/)
plane, plain (/pleɪn/)	*clause, claws* (/klɔːz/)
toe, tow (/təʊ/)	*cymbal, symbol* (/sɪmbəl/)
birth, berth (/bɜːθ/)	*due, dew* (/djuː/) [1]
I'll, aisle (/aɪl/)	*curb, kerb* (/kɜːb/) [2]

1 In American English, these words are pronounced without the /j/, and thus homophones with *do*.
2 In American English, these two words are both spelt *curb*.

Task 5.1 Stress marking (page 64) 

The stressed syllable is shown by the superscript tick in the following transcriptions:

absentee	/æbsən'tiː/	*phonetics*	/fə'netɪks/
assignment	/ə'saɪnmənt/	*primary*	/'praɪməri/
cassette	/kə'set/	*register*	/'redʒɪstə/
computer	/kəm'pjuːtə/	*revision*	/rɪ'vɪʒən/
dictionary	/'dɪkʃənəri/	*secondary*	/'sekəndəri/
essay	/'eseɪ/	*student*	/'stjuːdənt/
exam	/ɪg'zæm/	*thesaurus*	/θɪ'sɔːrəs/
grammar	/'græmə/	*tutor*	/'tjuːtə/
pencil	/'pensəl/	*vocabulary*	/və'kæbjʊləri/

Task 5.2 Stress in *-ity* words (page 65)

availability	/əveɪləb'ɪləti/	*impossibility*	/ɪmpɒsə'bɪləti/
Christianity	/krɪsti'ænəti/	*inferiority*	/ɪnfɪəri'ɒrəti/
complexity	/kəm'pleksəti/	*intensity*	/ɪn'tensəti/
confidentiality	/kɒnfɪdenʃi'æləti/	*majority*	/mə'dʒɒrəti/

equality	/ɪ'kwɒləti/	*nationality*	/næʃə'næləti/
extremity	/ɪk'streməti/	*personality*	/pɜːsə'næləti/
femininity	/femɪ'nɪnəti/	*popularity*	/pɒpjʊ'lærəti/
generosity	/dʒenə'rɒsəti/	*publicity*	/pʌ'blɪsəti/
humidity	/hjuː'mɪdəti/	*reality*	/ri'æləti/

The generalisation is that the stressed syllable is the one before the *-ity* suffix.

Task 5.3 Stress in -ic words 1 (page 65)

alcoholic	/ælkə'hɒlɪk/	*Islamic*	/ɪz'læmɪk/
algebraic	/ældʒɪ'breɪɪk/	*magnetic*	/mæg'netɪk/
alphabetic	/ælfə'betɪk/	*metallic*	/mə'tælɪk/
angelic	/æn'dʒelɪk/	*microscopic*	/maɪkrə'skɒpɪk/
atmospheric	/ætməs'ferɪk/	*optimistic*	/ɒptɪ'mɪstɪk/
atomic	/ə'tɒmɪk/	*organic*	/ɔː'gænɪk/
enthusiastic	/ɪnθjuːzi'æstɪk/	*photographic*	/fəʊtə'græfɪk/
historic	/hɪ'stɒrɪk/	*syllabic*	/sɪ'læbɪk/
idiotic	/ɪdi'ɒtɪk/	*titanic*	/taɪ'tænɪk/

The generalisation is that the stressed syllable is the one before the *-ic* suffix.

Task 5.4 Stress in *-ic* words 2 (page 65) 

The following words follow the generalisation, that is the stress is on the syllable before the final *-ic*:

acoustic, domestic, dramatic, Germanic, linguistic, pragmatic, prolific, terrific

The following words do not follow the generalisation. They all have stress on the first syllable.

Arabic, catholic, choleric, heretic, lunatic, rhetoric, turmeric

But notice the regularly stressed related forms *Arabica coffee* /ə'ræbɪkə/, *Catholicism* /kə'θɒlɪsɪzəm/, *heretical* /hə'retɪkəl/, *rhetorical* /rɪ'tɒrɪkəl/.

Task 5.5 Stress in -/ʃən/ words (page 66)

acceleration	/əkseləˈreɪʃən/
accommodation	/əkɒməˈdeɪʃən/
Alsatian	/ælˈseɪʃən/
coercion	/kəʊˈɜːʃən/
compassion	/kəmˈpæʃən/
comprehension	/kɒmprɪˈhenʃən/
constitution	/kɒnstɪˈtjuːʃən/
crustacean	/krʌˈsteɪʃən/
cushion	/ˈkʊʃən/
Dalmatian	/dælˈmeɪʃən/
expulsion	/ɪkˈspʌlʃən/
fashion	/ˈfæʃən/
generalisation	/dʒenrəlaɪˈzeɪʃən/
magician	/məˈdʒɪʃən/
mathematician	/mæθəməˈtɪʃən/
ocean	/ˈəʊʃən/
preposition	/prepəˈzɪʃən/
repercussion	/riːpəˈkʌʃən/
representation	/reprɪzenˈteɪʃən/
revolution	/revəˈluːʃən/
superstition	/suːpəˈstɪʃən/
suspicion	/səˈspɪʃən/
tuition	/tjuˈɪʃən/
Venetian	/vəˈniːʃən/

The generalisation is that the stressed syllable is the one before the /-ʃən/ suffix, regardless of how it is spelt.

There are two schools of thought about the value of stress rules in English. One says that there are so many exceptions to most rules that can be devised that they are not worth devoting time to; the stress placement in words should be learnt word-by-word from the dictionary. The other says that, even though there are exceptions, there are nonetheless underlying rules that, for instance, apply in new or invented words (for instance, how would you stress *rodentic*, a made-up word meaning 'to do with rodents'?). It seems worthwhile dealing with rules that cover over 90% of cases, as in Tasks 5.2, 5.3 and 5.5 above.

Task 5.6 The schwa vowel (page 67)

J~~a~~pan
Keny~~a~~
Finl~~a~~nd
Yem~~e~~n
J~~a~~maic~~a~~
Mon~~a~~co
B~~er~~mud~~a~~
Switz~~er~~l~~a~~nd
Th~~e~~ B~~a~~ham~~a~~s
Can~~a~~d~~a~~
M~~o~~rocco
Germ~~a~~ny
Gr~~e~~nad~~a~~
Leb~~a~~n~~o~~n
Arg~~e~~ntin~~a~~
M~~au~~rit~~iu~~s
Ven~~e~~zuel~~a~~
Th~~e~~ Neth~~er~~l~~a~~nds
Guat~~e~~mal~~a~~
Cost~~a~~ Ric~~a~~
Th~~e~~ Sol~~o~~m~~o~~n Isl~~a~~nds
West~~er~~n S~~a~~mo~~a~~

Task 5.7 Word-final schwa (page 68)

Some example words:

-a: *umbrella* /ʌmbrelə/, *arena* /əri:nə/, *Bermuda* /bəmju:də/
-ah: *verandah* /vərændə/, *cheetah* /tʃi:tə/, *Deborah* /debrə/ [1]
-ar: *vicar* /vɪkə/, *vinegar* /vɪnɪgə/, *calendar* /kæləndə/
-e: *genre* /ʒɒnrə/, *macabre* /məkɑ:brə/, *joie de vivre* /ʒwɑ: də vi:vrə/
-er: *teacher* /ti:tʃə/, *sister* /sɪstə/, *anger* /æŋgə/
-eur: *amateur* /æmətə/, *chauffeur* /ʃəʊfə/, *grandeur* /grændʒə/ [2]
-ire: *Cheshire* /tʃeʃə/, *Hampshire* /hæmpʃə/, *Yorkshire* /jɔ:kʃə/
-or: *doctor* /dɒktə/, *sailor* /seɪlə/, *error* /erə/
-ough: *thorough* /θʌrə/, *Middlesbrough* /mɪdəlzbrə/, *Peterborough* /pi:təbrə/
-our: *harbour* /hɑ:bə/, *colour* /kʌlə/, *honour* /ɒnə/ [3]
-re: *centre* /sentə/, *theatre* /θɪətə/, *meagre* /mi:gə/ [4]
-ur: *murmur* /mɜ:mə/, *Arthur* /ɑ:θə/, *sulphur* /sʌlfə/
-ure: *nature* /neɪtʃə/, *figure* /fɪgə/, *leisure* /leʒə/
-yr: *martyr* /mɑ:tə/, *satyr* /sætə/, *zephyr* /zefə/

1 Some of these words can also be spelt without the *h*, for example *Debra, veranda*.
2 Some speakers pronounce these French loanwords with stress (and therefore not schwa) on the final syllable.
3 Americans spell these words without the *u*, that is the same as set 8: *harbor, color, honor*.
4 Americans spell these with final *-er*, that is the same as set 5: *center, theater, meager*.

Task 6.1 Analysing syllable structure (page 73)

	Onset	Peak	Coda	Cluster?
two	t	u:		No
step	st	e	p	Initial /st/
sails	s	eɪ	lz	Final /lz/
thank	θ	æ	ŋk	Final /ŋk/
once	w	ʌ	ns	Final /ns/
phoned	f	əʊ	nd	Final /nd/
sprint	spr	ɪ	nt	Initial /spr/, final /nt/

mixed	m	ɪ	kst	Final /kst/
eye		aɪ		No
quirk	kw	ɜː	k	Initial /kw/
voiced	v	ɔɪ	st	Final /st/
write	r	aɪ	t	No
through	θr	uː		Initial /θr/
schools	sk	uː	lz	Initial /sk/, final /lz/
twelfths	tw	e	lfθs	Initial /tw/, final /lfθs/
washed	w	ɒ	ʃt	Final /ʃt/
eight		eɪ	t	No
yacht	j	ɒ	t	No
flex	fl	e	ks	Initial /fl/, final /ks/
gnome	n	əʊ	m	No

Task 6.2 Alliteration in similes (page 74)

Notice that many of these similes make little sense nowadays. Consult a big dictionary to find out their origin.

as busy as a bee /biː/
(or *beaver* /biːvə/)
as dead as a dodo /dəʊdəʊ/
(or *doornail* /dɔːneɪl/)
as proud as a peacock /piːkɒk/
as fit as a fiddle /fɪdəl/
as bold as brass /brɑːs/
as good as gold /gəʊld/
as cool as a cucumber /kjuːkʌmbə/
as still as a statue /stætjuː/
(or *stone* /stəʊn/)

as pretty as a picture /pɪktʃə/
as large as life /laɪf/
as bright as a button /bʌtən/
as mad as a March hare /mɑːtʃ heə/ [1]
as pleased as Punch /pʌntʃ/ [2]
as blind as a bat /bæt/
as thick as thieves /θiːvz/
as right as rain /reɪn/
as green as grass /grɑːs/
as plump as a partridge /pɑːtrɪdʒ/

1 March is the breeding season for hares
2 Of Punch and Judy fame

In Tasks 6.2, 6.3 and 6.6, you are helped by being given the first half of the expression, so that you only have to complete it. This is a less daunting task than being asked to supply the whole expression. The emphasis here is on alliteration and rhyme, not on the depth of your vocabulary.

Task 6.3 Alliteration in fixed expressions (page 75)

Again, consult a good dictionary if you do not know any of these expressions.

this and that /ðæt/
rough and ready /redi/
spick and span /spæn/
hale and hearty /hɑːti/
jump for joy /dʒɔɪ/
back to basics /beɪsɪks/
beat about the bush /bʊʃ/
two peas in a pod /pɒd/
go against the grain /greɪn/
mind over matter /mætə/
add fuel to the fire /faɪə/
(or *flames* /fleɪmz/)
not on your nelly /neli/
put your money where your mouth /maʊθ/ *is*

better safe than sorry /sɒri/
through thick and thin /θɪn/
part and parcel /pɑːsəl/
risk life and limb /lɪm/
without a worry /wʌri/ *in the world* /wɜːld/
live in the lap /læp/ *of luxury* /lʌkʃəri/
tricks of the trade /treɪd/
in dribs and drabs /dræbz/
His bark is worse than his bite /baɪt/
Where's there's a will /wɪl/, *there's a way* /weɪ/
It takes two /tuː/ *to tango* /tæŋgəʊ/

Task 6.4 Searching for rhymes (pages 76 and 77) 

The correct route is:

great /greɪt/, *date* /deɪt/
flood /flʌd/, *mud* /mʌd/
word /wɜːd/, *bird* /bɜːd/
sword /sɔːd/, *ward* /wɔːd/
wear /weə/, *care* /keə/
enough /ɪnʌf/, *stuff* /stʌf/

shoot /ʃuːt/, *boot* /buːt/
any /eni/, *penny* /peni/
laugh /lɑːf/, *graph* /grɑːf/
mix /mɪks/, *sticks* /stɪks/
calm /kɑːm/, *charm* /tʃɑːm/
pretty /prɪti/, *city* /sɪti/

Task 6.5 Limericks (page 78) 

There was a young hunter named Shepherd /ʃepəd/
Who was eaten for lunch by a leopard /lepəd/
Said the leopard, replete, /rɪpliːt/
'He'd have gone down a treat /triːt/
If he had been salted and peppered!' /pepəd/

There was a young man from Darjeeling /dɑːdʒiːlɪŋ/
Who got on the bus for West Ealing. /iːlɪŋ/
It said on the door /dɔː/
'Don't spit on the floor.' /flɔː/
So he stood up and spat on the ceiling. /siːlɪŋ/

There was a big 'keeper called Walter /wɔːltə/
Who played on the island of Malta. /mɔːltə/
But his kicks were so long /lɒŋ/
And the wind was so strong, /strɒŋ/
That the ball ended up in Gibraltar. /dʒɪbrɔːltə/

There was a young player from Clyde /klaɪd/
Took a penalty kick that went wide. /waɪd/
The next week his brother /brʌðə/
Squandered another. /ənʌðə/
Now neither can get in the side. /saɪd/

There was a young striker from Reading [1] /redɪŋ/
Bumped his brow on a door at a wedding. /wedɪŋ/
It made his head swell, /swel/
But he said 'Just as well, /wel/
'Cos now I'll improve on my heading.' /hedɪŋ/

There was a reserve from Man U /juː/
Who seldom had much work to do. /duː/
For a half-hour or so /səʊ/
He'd run to and fro /frəʊ/
Then reverse it and run fro and to. /tuː/

A striker from A C Milan /mɪlæn/
Wrote poems that just wouldn't scan. /skæn/
When told this was so, /səʊ/
He said, 'Yes, I know, /nəʊ/
But I always try to get as many syllables into the last line as I possibly can.' /kæn/

1 The town *Reading* is pronounced /redɪŋ/, as opposed to the verbal form *reading* /riːdɪŋ/.

In addition to the humour, rhymes such as limericks also emphasise the rhythmic nature of speech. Students can be set the task of creating their own limericks, given a first line, such as *There was an old teacher named Brown*.

Task 6.6 Reduplication (page 80)

The following reduplications involve alternation of the vowel:

chit-chat, flip-flop, hip-hop, hoo-ha, knick-knack, mish-mash, pitter-patter, seesaw, tip-top, wishy-washy, shipshape, bric-a-brac

The following reduplications involve alternation of the initial consonant(s):

arty-farty, chock-a-block, fuddy-duddy, hanky-panky, hocus-pocus, hotchpotch, hurly-burly, itsy-bitsy, mumbo-jumbo, culture vulture, flower power, from hero to zero, gender bender, rich bitch

If you are not familiar with any of these expressions, look them up in a good dictionary.

Task 6.7 Vicars' knickers (page 81)

right site /raɪt saɪt/
fake ache /feɪk eɪk/
cheap jeep /tʃiːp dʒiːp/
six kicks /sɪks kɪks/
new glue /njuː gluː/
vile style /vaɪl staɪl/
four more /fɔː mɔː/
wax tracks /wæks træks/
beef thief /biːf θiːf/
Greek freak /griːk friːk/

frayed suede /freɪd sweɪd/
main vein /meɪn veɪn/
whose cruise /huːz kruːz/
dry pie /draɪ paɪ/
stewed food /stjuːd fuːd/
lone groan /ləʊn grəʊn/ or *moan* /məʊn/
tanned hand /tænd hænd/
blurred bird /blɜːd bɜːd/
mute newt /mjuːt njuːt/
wise ties /waɪz taɪz/

dire choir /daɪə kwaɪə/
metal kettle /metəl ketəl/
pretty kitty /prɪti kɪti/
woolly bully /wʊli bʊli/

green sardine /griːn sɑːdiːn/
obese niece /əbiːs niːs/
tipsy gypsy /tɪpsi dʒɪpsi/
better sweater /betə swetə/

dreary theory /drɪəri θɪəri/
young tongue /jʌŋ tʌŋ/
funky monkey /fʌŋki mʌŋki/
killer gorilla /kɪlə gərɪlə/
quirky turkey /kwɜːki tɜːki/
lunar crooner /luːnə kruːnə/

swan's bronze /swɒnz brɒnz/
scarier area /skeəriə(r) eəriə/
Ukraine champagne /juːkreɪn ʃæmpeɪn/
starry safari /stɑːri səfɑːri/
nocturnal colonel /nɒktɜːnəl kɜːnəl/
deceased priest /dɪsiːst priːst/

great weight /greɪt weɪt/
giant client /dʒaɪənt klaɪənt/
huge stooge /hjuːdʒ stuːdʒ/

colossal fossil /kəlɒsəl fɒsəl/
humungous fungus /hjuːmʌŋgəs fʌŋgəs/

Task 6.8 Spoonerisms (page 85)

Actual utterance	Intended utterance	Transcription	Transposed consonants
Slips attributed to Spooner			
Is the bean dizzy?	*Is the Dean busy?*	/diːn bɪzi/	/d, b/
Ye noble tons of soil.	*Ye noble sons of toil.*	/sʌnz tɔɪl/	/s, t/
we'll have hags flung out	*we'll have flags hung out*	/flægz hʌŋ/	/fl, h/
May I sew you to another sheet?	*May I show you to another seat?*	/ʃəʊ siːt/	/ʃ, s/
a nosy little cook	*a cosy little nook*	/kəʊzi nʊk/	/k, n/
The weight of rages	*The rate of wages*	/reɪt weɪdʒɪz/	/r, w/
a shoving leopard	*a loving shepherd*	/lʌvɪŋ ʃepəd/	/l, ʃ/
beery wenches	*weary benches*	/wɪəri bentʃɪz/	/w, b/
fighting a liar	*lighting a fire*	/laɪtɪŋ faɪə/	/l, f/
a blushing crow	*a crushing blow*	/krʌʃɪŋ bləʊ/	/kr, bl/
chase the train of thought	*trace the chain of thought*	/treɪs tʃeɪn/	/tr, tʃ/
hissed all my mystery lectures	*missed all my History lectures*	/mɪst hɪstəri/	/m, h/
tasted two worms	*wasted two terms*	/weɪstɪd tɜːmz/	/w, t/

rags and bugs	*rugs and bags*	/rʌgz bægz/	/ʌ, æ/ [1]
the town drain	*the down train* [2]	/daʊn treɪn/	/d, t/

Modern, invented spoonerisms

shake a tower	*take a shower*	/teɪk ʃaʊə/	/t, ʃ/
very mad banners	*very bad manners*	/bæd mænəz/	/b, m/
roaring with pain	*pouring with rain*	/pɔːrɪŋ reɪn/	/p, r/
Wave the sails	*Save the whales*	/seɪv weɪlz/	/s, w/
my bunny phone	*my funny bone*	/fʌni bəʊn/	/f, b/
crawls through the fax	*falls through the cracks*	/fɔːlz kræks/	/f, kr/
go help me sod	*so help me God*	/səʊ gɒd/	/s, g/
monk jail	*junk mail*	/dʒʌŋk meɪl/	/dʒ, m/
a damp stealer	*a stamp dealer*	/stæmp diːlə/	/st, d/
a lack of pies	*a pack of lies*	/pæk laɪz/	/p, l/
keys and parrots	*peas and carrots*	/piːz kærəts/	/p, k/
belly jeans	*jelly beans*	/dʒeli biːnz/	/dʒ, b/
Sale of Two Titties	*Tale of Two Cities*	/teɪl sɪtɪz/	/t, s/

1 A transposition of vowels
2 The down train is the train from London. The juxtaposition of these four spoonerisms in such close proximity makes one very suspicious of their authenticity.

Task 6.9 What's the difference between ... ? (page 86)

Q: What's the difference between a prince and the water in a fountain?
A: A prince is the heir to the throne. Water in a fountain is thrown to the air. /θrəʊn, eə/

Q: What's the difference between a man who has visited Niagara Falls, and one who has not?
A: A man who has visited Niagara Falls has seen a mist. One who has not has missed a scene. /mɪst, siːn/

Q: What's the difference between a cat and a comma?
A: A cat has claws at the end of its paws. A comma is a pause at the end of a clause. /pɔːz, klɔːz/

Q: What's the difference between a married man and a bachelor?
A: A married man kisses his Mrs. A bachelor misses his kisses. /mɪsɪz, kɪsɪz/

Q: What's the difference between a mouldy lettuce and a dismal song?
A: A mouldy lettuce is a bad salad. A dismal song is a sad ballad. /bæd, sæləd, sæd, bæləd/

Q: What's the difference between a cuddle and a louse?
A: A cuddle is a bear hug. A louse is a hair bug. /beə, hʌg, heə, bʌg/

Q: What's the difference between a hostile audience and a sick cow?
A: A hostile audience boos madly. A sick cow moos badly. /buːz, mædli, muːz, bædli/

Q: What's the difference between a squeaking hinge and eggs for breakfast?
A: A squeaking hinge begs to be oiled. The other is eggs to be boiled. /begz, ɔɪld, egz, bɔɪld/

Q: What's the difference between sticky tape and a stableboy?
A: Sticky tape mends a tear. A stableboy tends a mare. /mendz, teə, tendz, meə/

Q: What's the difference between a marksman and a loose-bowelled owl?
A: A marksman shoots and hits. A loose-bowelled owl hoots and sh*ts! /ʃuːts, hɪts, huːts, ʃɪts/

Q: What's the difference between a coyote and a flea?
A: A coyote howls on the prairie. A flea prowls on the hairy. /haʊlz, preəri, praʊlz, heəri/

Q: What's the difference between a fisherman and a lazy schoolboy?
A: A fisherman baits his hooks. A lazy schoolboy hates his books. /beɪts, hʊks, heɪts, bʊks/

Task 6.10 Pig Latin (page 89) 

1 *Do you know what this says?* /duː [1] juː nəʊ wɒt ðɪs sez/

2 *Your dog bit my leg.* /jɔː dɒg bɪt maɪ leg/

3 *My wife writes kids books.* /maɪ waɪf raɪts kɪdz bʊks/

4 *Thank you very much.* /θæŋk juː veri mʌtʃ/

5 *Please study harder for your coming test.* /pliːz stʌdi hɑːdə fɔː [1] jɔː kʌmɪŋ test/

6 *The swimming pool is quite cold.* /ðiː [1] swɪmɪŋ puːl ɪz kwaɪt kəʊld/

7 *You can play all day with Ray.* /juː kæn [1] pleɪ ɔːl deɪ wɪð reɪ/

8 *Why not buy a bigger bag?* /waɪ nɒt baɪ eɪ [1] bɪgə bæg/

1 These words would normally have /ə/ in connected speech.

Limericks, spoonerisms and Pig Latin can all be found on the internet, by typing those words into a search engine. They can then be used in tasks. But beware: some examples on the internet do not scan or rhyme properly. The internet is, after all, unregulated.

Task 6.11 Syllable anagrams (page 89)

department /dɪpɑːtmənt/
roundabout /raʊndəbaʊt/
computer /kəmpjuːtə/
performance /pəfɔːməns/
photograph /fəʊtəgrɑːf/
world-famous /wɜːldfeɪməs/
inscription /ɪnskrɪpʃən/
magnetism /mægnətɪzəm/
thought-provoking /θɔːtprəvəʊkɪŋ/
university /juːnɪvɜːsəti/

It is surprisingly difficult to write examples for syllable anagrams, because in many words there is disagreement over where syllables begin and end; for instance, whether a particular consonant is final in the first syllable or initial in the second (or even, as a more radical analysis may have it, belongs to both syllables). Dictionaries that use a superscript tick to mark stress have to commit themselves to specifying exactly where the stressed syllable begins. The *Collins Cobuild Advanced Learner's English Dictionary* avoids this problem by underlining the vowel of the stressed syllable. It is worth reading the syllabification sections in the introductions to the *Longman*

Pronunciation Dictionary and *Cambridge Pronouncing Dictionary*, in order to understand the depth of this problem and the different analyses that could be applied.

Task 7.3 Phonemic Boggle (page 94)

Phonemic Boggle game 1

Transcription	Spelling	Transcription	Spelling
/æs/	*ass*	/sæst/	*sassed* [6]
/æst/	*assed* [1]	/sæt/	*sat*
/æt/	*at*	/skæt/	*scat* [7]
/ækæk/	*ack-ack* [2]	/stæk/	*stack*
/æks/	*axe*	/stæks/	*stacks, stack's, stacks'*
/ækst/	*axed*		
/ækt/	*act*	/stækt/	*stacked*
/ækts/	*acts*	/stæts/	*stats* [8]
/kæt/	*cat*	/tæk/	*tack*
/kæts/	*cats, cat's, cats'*	/tæks/	*tacks, tack's, tacks', tax*
/sæk/	*sack, sac* [3]		
/sæks/	*sacks, sack's, sacks', sacs* [3]*, sac's, sacs', sax* [4]	/tækst/	*taxed*
		/tækt/	*tacked, tact*
		/tæs/	*Tass* [9]
/sækt/	*sacked*	/tæt/	*tat* [10 11]
/sæs/	*sass* [5]	/tæts/	*tats* [11]

1 As in *He assed about* 'He acted foolishly' (especially in American English)
2 An abbreviation of *anti-aircraft gun*
3 A botanical term for a part of a plant that looks like a bag and may contain liquid
4 A common abbreviation for *saxophone*
5 'Talk or behaviour that is rude or lacking respect' (especially in American English)
6 As in *He sassed his father* 'He talked rudely to his father' (especially in American English)
7 (i) An exclamation, meaning 'Shoo!', (ii) 'a type of jazz singing that uses words with no meaning' (popularised by singers such as Louis Armstrong and Ella Fitzgerald), (iii) 'animal excrement' (especially in American English)
8 A common abbreviation of *statistics*
9 The Russian news *agency* (www.tass.net)

10 (i) 'anything that looks cheap, is of low quality or in bad condition', (ii) as in *tit-for-tat*
11 (Verb) 'a kind of crochet'

It may have become obvious to you that:

- More words are possible, if we take American pronunciation into account, eg *cast* and *ask* are pronounced /kæst, æsk/ in American English.
- There are two reasons why the number of words we created is so large. Firstly, /s/ is often a suffix for plural nouns, third person present tense verbs, and possessives. Secondly, /t/ is often a suffix for past tenses and participles.

Phonemic Boggle game 2

Transcription	Spelling	Transcription	Spelling
/ɒks/	*ox*	/sɒts/	*sots* [3], *sot's, sots'*
/kɒk/	*cock*	/skɒt/	*Scot, Scott*
/kɒks/	*cocks, cock's, cocks', cox* [1]	/skɒts/	*Scots, Scot's, Scots', Scotts, Scott's, Scotts'*
/kɒkt/	*cocked*		
/kɒkst/	*coxed* [1]	/stɒk/	*stock*
/kɒst/	*cost*	/stɒks/	*stocks, stock's, stocks'*
/kɒsts/	*costs, cost's, costs'*		
/kɒt/	*cot*	/stɒkt/	*stocked*
/kɒts/	*cots, cot's, cots'*	/tɒk/	*tock* [4]
/sɒk/	*sock* [2]	/tɒs/	*toss*
/sɒks/	*socks* [2], *sock's, socks'*	/tɒst/	*tossed*
/sɒkt/	*socked* [2]	/tɒt/	*tot*
/sɒt/	*sot* [3]	/tɒts/	*tots, tot's, tots'*

1 (Noun) 'the person who steers a rowing boat', (verb) 'to steer a rowing boat'
2 (Verb, slang) 'to hit', as in *He socked me in the eye*
3 'A drunkard'
4 As in *tick-tock*, the sound of a clock

Task 7.4 Phonemic word chains (page 95)

/kɪs/	*kiss*	/ruːm/	*room*
/kɪk/	*kick*	/wuːm/	*womb*
/tʃɪk/	*chick*	/wɔːm/	*warm*
/tʃiːk/	*cheek*	/wɔːl/	*wall*
/rɪns/	*rinse*	/steɪdʒ/	*stage*
/mɪns/	*mince*	/steɪt/	*state*
/mɪnt/	*mint*	/sleɪt/	*slate*
/ment/	*meant*	/pleɪt/	*plate*
/went/	*went*	/plaɪt/	*plight*
/wɒnt/	*want*	/flaɪt/	*flight*
/wɒʃt/	*washed*	/fraɪt/	*fright*
/weɪst/	*waist*	/klɑːs/	*class*
/peɪst/	*paste*	/klɑːk/	*clerk*
/peɪnt/	*paint*	/klɪk/	*click*
/seɪnt/	*saint*	/klɪp/	*clip*
/sent/	*scent*	/slɪp/	*slip*
/bent/	*bent*	/skɪp/	*skip*
/bend/	*bend*	/skɪl/	*skill*
/bænd/	*band*	/skuːl/	*school*

These word chains are not as easy to create as they might seem. You need to choose a start word and an end word that have the same syllable structure, for example *waist* and *band* are both CVCC. Then see what the fewest number of changes is, to go from one to the other. Finally, you need to give clues to the missing words.

Task 7.6 Phonemic Wordsearch (page 98)

Here are the names with their transcriptions. If you are not familiar with these personalities, visit the websites given below.

Dan Aykroyd	/dæn/	dan.elwood.net/aykroyd
Judy Blume	/dʒuːdi/	judyblume.com
Jeff Bridges	/dʒef/	jeffbridges.com
David Copperfield	/deɪvɪd/	dcopperfield.com
Cindy Crawford	/sɪndi/	cindy.com
Vin Diesel	/vɪn/	art-of-vin-diesel.com
Michael Jackson	/maɪkəl/	michaeljackson.com

Mick Jagger	/mɪk/	mickjagger.com
Don Johnson	/dɒn/ [1]	donjohnson.cjb.net
Nicole Kidman	/nɪkəʊl/	teamnicole.com
Jude Law	/dʒuːd/ [2]	londonblue.net
John Lennon	/dʒɒn/	lennon.net
Jennifer Lopez	/dʒenɪfə/	jenniferlopez.com
Nelson Mandela	/nelsən/	anc.org.za/people/mandela.html
Richard Nixon	/rɪtʃəd/	presidentsusa.net/nixon.html
Nick Nolte	/nɪk/ [3]	members.aol.com/wienerdox/page
Monica Seles	/mɒnɪkə/	monica-seles.com
Rod Stewart	/rɒd/	rodstewart.com
Sue Townsend	/suː/	bbc.co.uk/arts/books/author/townsend
Madonna	/mədɒnə/	home.madonna.com
Bruce Willis	/bruːs/	brucewillis.com

1 overlaps with Madonna
2 overlaps with Judy
3 overlaps with Monica

Good wordsearches that work on spelling (that is, where there are a large number of words in a small square) are, in fact, difficult to create. I suggest you use ones found in magazines. Well-crafted wordsearches that work on phonemic transcription, such as Task 7.6, are even more difficult.

Task 7.7 Phonemic crosswords (page 100)

Crossword 1

1 s	əʊ	2 k
ɔɪ	■	ɑː
3 l	eɪ	m

The words in spelling:
Across: 1 *soak*, 3 *lame*.
Down: 1 *soil*, 2 *calm*.

Crossword 2

■	■	1 r	aɪ	2 m
■	■	æ	■	uː
3 k	ʌ	b	ə	d
ʊ	■	ɪ	■	■
4 d	eɪ	t	■	■

The words in spelling:
Across: 1 *rhyme,* 3 *cupboard,* 4 *date.*
Down: 1 *rabbit,* 2 *mood,* 3 *could.*

Crossword 3

1 h	ɜː	2 b	■	■
aɪ	■	e	■	■
3 k	e	n	ɪ	4 θ
■	■	ɪ	■	ɔː
5 d	ɪ	f	iː	t
e	■	ɪ	■	■
6 k	ɔː	t	■	■

The words in spelling:
Across: 1 *herb,* 3 *Kenneth,* 5 *defeat,* 6 *court.*
Down: 1 *hike,* 2 *benefit,* 4 *thought,* 5 *deck.*

Crossword 4

1 p	aɪ	2 l	ə	3 t			4 s	k	5 r	æ	6 p
ɜː		æ		7 æ	s	e	t		ʊə		ɔː
8 p	ʌ	t	ɪ	ŋ			9 ʌ	p	r	aɪ	t
ə		ɪ		10 k	ɑː	s	t		ə		ə
11 s	12 e	n	13 s	ə			14 ə	15 b	l	16 eɪ	z
	d		e					r		k	
	ɪ		n					eɪ		ɪ	
17 s	t	18 ɑː	t	19 ə			20 k	l	21 ɪ	ŋ	22 z
p		k		23 f	r	ɪ	l		n		e
24 l	ɪ	t	ə	l			25 æ	d	v	ɜː	b
ɪ		ɪ		26 əʊ	n	ɪ	ŋ		ɔɪ		r
27 t	e	k	s	t			28 k	əʊ	s	t	ə

The words in spelling:

Across: 1 *pilot,* 4 *scrap,* 7 *asset,* 8 *putting,* 9 *upright,* 10 *cast,* 11 *censor,* 14 *ablaze,* 17 *starter,* 20 *clings,* 23 *frill,* 24 *little,* 25 *adverb,* 26 *owning,* 27 *text,* 28 *coaster.*

Down: 1 *purpose,* 2 *Latin,* 3 *tanker,* 4 *stutter,* 5 *rural,* 6 *porters,* 12 *edit,* 13 *cent,* 15 *Braille,* 16 *aching,* 17 *split,* 18 *Arctic,* 19 *afloat,* 20 *clank,* 21 *invoice,* 22 *zebra.*

It is not difficult to create small phonemic crosswords, like 1, 2 and 3 above. You will find it is easier if the intersecting squares are consonant sounds, rather than vowels. However, it is very difficult to create larger, symmetrical ones like 4.

Further reading and websites

Chapter 1 Consonant and vowel sounds

For a detailed description of how the vowels and consonants are pronounced, and problems in analysing phonemes, see any good introductory phonetics book, such as Roach (2000) and Cruttenden (2001). For a description of how vowels and consonants vary across accents worldwide, see Wells (1982).

The most comprehensive book on the correspondences between sounds and spellings of British English is Carney (1994). Also see Carney (1997).

For online materials that teach phonetics (including vowels and consonants):

www.phon.ucl.ac.uk/resource/tutorials.html#phon

For free downloadable phonemic/phonetic symbol fonts that can be used with word-processing programs on your computer:

www.phon.ucl.ac.uk/shop/fonts.php

Chapter 2 Background

On the properties of human language that distinguish it from animal languages, see Yule (1996: Chaps. 3 & 4). The differences in grammar between spoken and written language are discussed in detail by Biber, Finegan, Conrad, Johansson and Leech (1999). Lyons (1981: §1.4) goes into the various reasons why spoken language is considered to have priority over written language.

The different writing systems used by languages past and present are described by Crystal (1987: Chap. 33). Crystal (1995: Chap. 18) gives an in-depth analysis of the development of English spelling.

On varieties of English worldwide, and the influence of British English around the world, see Crystal (1997), McArthur (1998) and Bauer (2002).

Chapter 3 Minimal pairs

The following website gives all the minimal pairs for all the permutations of English phonemes (vowels and consonants):
www.marlodge.supanet.com/wordlist/index.html

Chapter 4 Homophones and homographs

The following websites list all the homophones and homographs of English:
www.marlodge.supanet.com/wordlist/homophon.html
www.marlodge.supanet.com/wordlist/homogrph.html

Chapter 5 Stress and schwa

Introductory phonetics books such as Roach (2000: Chaps. 9–11) and Cruttenden (2001: Chap. 10) cover the main points of stress, listing many rules regarding stress placement.

Chapter 6 Syllable structure

Hayter (1977) is an account of the life and times of Rev Spooner.
For limericks: www.teachingideas.co.uk/english/limerick.htm
For Pig Latin: www.idioma-software.com/pig/pig_latin.html

Chapter 7 Practice tasks

Books that contain tasks on transcription and familiarisation with symbols (but a lot besides) include Bowen and Marks (1992), Hancock (1995), Garcia Lecumberri and Maidment (2000) and Vaughan-Rees (2002).

Chapter 9 Literacy and spelling reform

Crystal (1995: Chaps. 18 & 23) covers both these aspects of language.

On literacy, see Kern (2000) and Holme (2004). UNESCO's Institute for Statistics (www.uis.unesco.org) compiles literacy statistics and estimates for countries of the world. Countries conspicuous by the absence of their figures include the UK, the USA, Canada, Australia and New Zealand.

For online literacy games:
www.bbc.co.uk/schools/4_11/literacy.shtml

On spelling reform: www.spellingsociety.org

References

Asmah Haji Omar (1989). The Malay spelling reform. *Journal of the Simplified Spelling Society* (UK), 3(2), 9–13.

Bauer, L. (2002). *An introduction to international varieties of English.* Edinburgh: Edinburgh University Press.

Bell, M. (2001). *Why English spelling should be updated.* [Pamphlet] UK: Simplified Spelling Society.

Biber, D., Finegan, E., Conrad, S., Johansson, S. & Leech, G. (1999). *The Longman grammar of spoken and written English.* New York: Longman.

Bowen, T. & Marks, J. (1992). *The pronunciation book.* London: Longman.

Brown, A. (1996) The trouble with spelling. *Speak Out!* (Newsletter of the IATEFL Pronunciation Special Interest Group) 17, 23–30.

Carney, E. (1994). *A survey of English spelling.* London and New York: Routledge.

Carney, E. (1997). *English spelling.* London and New York: Routledge.

Chomsky, N. & Halle, M. (1968). *The sound pattern of English.* New York: Harper & Row.

Collins Cobuild Advanced Learner's English Dictionary (ed. Sinclair, J. 2003, 4th ed.) London: HarperCollins.

Cruttenden, A. (2001). *Gimson's pronunciation of English.* (6th ed.) London: Edward Arnold.

Crystal, D. (1987). *The Cambridge encyclopedia of language.* Cambridge and New York: Cambridge University Press.

Crystal, D. (1995). *The Cambridge encyclopedia of the English language.* Cambridge: Cambridge University Press.

Crystal, D. (1997). *English as a global language.* New York: Cambridge University Press.

Dewan Bahasa dan Pustaka (1981) *Daftar ejaan rumi Bahasa Malaysia.* Kuala Lumpur: Dewan Bahasa dan Pustaka.

Fry, D. B. (1947). The frequency of occurrence of speech sounds in southern English. *Archives Néerlandaises de Phonétique Expérimentale* 20.

Garcia Lecumberri, M. L. & Maidment, J. A. (2000). *English transcription course.* London: Arnold.

Goulandris, N. K. (1994) Teaching spelling: bridging theory and practice. In G. D. A. Brown & N. C. Ellis (Eds.) *Handbook of spelling: Theory, process and intervention* (pp. 407–23). New York: John Wiley.

Hancock, M. (1995). *Pronunciation games.* Cambridge: Cambridge University Press.

Hayter, W. G. (1977). *Spooner: A biography.* London: W H Allen.

Holme, R. (2004). *Literacy: An introduction.* Edinburgh: Edinburgh University Press.

International Phonetic Association (Eds. 1999) *Handbook of the International Phonetic Association.* Cambridge: Cambridge University Press.

Kern, R. (2000). *Literacy and language teaching.* Oxford: Oxford University Press.

Lennox, C. & Siegel, L. S. (1994) The role of phonological and orthographic processes in learning to spell. In G. D. A. Brown & N. C. Ellis (Eds.) *Handbook of spelling: Theory, process and intervention* (pp. 93–109). New York: John Wiley.

Lyons, J. (1981). *Language and linguistics: An introduction.* Cambridge and New York: Cambridge University Press.

McArthur, T. (1998). *The English languages.* New York: Cambridge University Press.

Roach, P. (2000). *English phonetics and phonology: A practical course.* (3rd ed.) Cambridge: Cambridge University Press.

Roach, P., Hartman, J. & Setter, J. (Eds. 2003) [Daniel Jones] *English pronouncing dictionary.* (16th ed.) Cambridge & New York: Cambridge University Press.

Strevens, P. (1980) *Teaching English as an international language.* Oxford: Pergamon.

Townsend, S. (1984) *The growing pains of Adrian Mole.* London: Penguin.

Vaughan-Rees, M. (2002). *Test your pronunciation.* Harlow: Penguin/Pearson.

Wells, J. C. (1982). *Accents of English.* Cambridge and New York: Cambridge University Press.

Wells, J. C. (2000) *Longman Pronunciation Dictionary.* (2nd ed.) Harlow: Pearson Education.

Yule, G. (1996). *The study of language.* (2nd ed.) Cambridge and New York: Cambridge University Press.

Contents of the CD

Track	Task	Page	Title
1		vii	Symbols for British English phonemes: vowels
2		vii	Symbols for British English phonemes: consonants
3	1.1	8	Searching for sound types A
4	1.1	8	Searching for sound types B
5	1.1	9	Searching for sound types C
6	1.1	9	Searching for sound types D
7	1.1	9	Searching for sound types E
8	1.1	9	Searching for sound types F
9	1.2	9, 10	Searching for /j/ words
10	1.3	9, 11	Searching for /g/ words
11	1.4	19	Transcription to spelling 1
12	1.6	20	Transcription to spelling 2
13	1.7	20, 21	Searching for /e/ words
14	1.8	22	Transcription to spelling 3
15	1.9	22, 23	Searching for /ɑː/ words